Product Development for the Lean Enterprise

Why Toyota's System is Four Times More Productive and How You Can Implement It

D0253515

About the Author

Michael N. Kennedy has pioneered the redesign of organizational processes for over 35 years. During his 30 years at Texas Instruments, Mr. Kennedy was the lead engineer on many developmental projects including both missile system products and manufacturing systems. He was credited as being not only an exceptional design engineer but also as a leader in developing and applying the initial concepts of concurrent engineering. During his last ten years at TI, he led the integration of manufacturing and development systems at a major TI facility. He also developed the strategy across the defense business sector for design automation in concert with a redesigned product development environment. In addition to his role as a leader in systems development within TI, Mr. Kennedy also was active in collaborative sharing across the country including many consortia based projects and presentations at engineering and manufacturing conferences.

As a consultant, Mr. Kennedy works extensively with the National Center for Manufacturing Sciences and with major manufacturing companies, including General Motors, United Technologies, Allied Signal, and Delphi, to assess and advance American product development systems. His efforts also have included an extensive nationwide benchmarking study examining a broad spectrum of manufacturing companies in an effort to find unique and effective product development methodologies.

Product Development for the Lean Enterprise

Why Toyota's System is Four Times More Productive and How You Can Implement It

by

Michael N. Kennedy

RICHMOND, VIRGINIA

ISBN 10: 1-892538-18-0
ISBN 13: 978-1-892538-18-5

If your bookseller does not have this book in stock,
it can be ordered directly from the publisher.
Contact us for information about discounts
on quantity purchases.

The Oaklea Press
6912 Three Chopt Road, Suite B
Richmond, Virginia 23226

Voice: 1-800-295-4066
Facsimile: 1-804-281-5686
Email: Info@OakleaPress.com

This book can be purchased online at
http://www.LeanTransformation.com

Acknowledgements

The ideas and concepts presented in this book coalesced in my mind over the last ten years based largely on my interactions with many people dedicated to improving product development methodologies. I listened, learned, and together we continually challenged existing ways of developing products.

The members of the NCMS project that was the basis for the conclusions in this book were individually instrumental for formulating the conclusions. I owe a debt of gratitude to Mike Gnam of NCMS, Ern Mink and Vijay Srinivas of Delphi, John Convey and Suzanne Carlaw of Ortech, Mark Adkins of Cincinnati Milacron, Gordon Brunner and Tim Bell of UTC Automotive, David Cameron of TI, and Leslie Interrante and Dennis Anderson of Sandia.

I owe special thanks to Dr. Allen Ward. Much of the technical content concerning the principles of Toyota was developed by Dr. Ward and his colleagues. He taught these principles to our NCMS project and personally mentored me in my adapting these principles within my overall view of product development and change.

I would also like to recognize a number of colleagues who volunteered their time to read, challenge, and critique the manuscript during development. Their thoughts contributed greatly to the technical content of the book. They were Dick Weber, Mike Gnam, Emery Powell, John Convey, Fred Eintracht, and Dale Henning.

In addition, I'd like to acknowledge my years at Texas Instruments. TI, as a company, has always been open to change and provided a great environment for challenging and developing new technologies and process methodologies. In particular, Bill Lawrence, Steve Douthit, Allan Hrncir, Robin LeoGrande, Greg

Tucker, Jay Goode, Jim Shiflett, and Karl Arunski all were inspirations behind many of the positive characters depicted in the book.

I would also like to thank Patricia E. Moody, the author of many books of her own, for taking an interest in this project and for guiding me through the publishing process, and to Stephen Hawley Martin, publisher of The Oaklea Press, for his personal help in making the book a reality.

And certainly, there is my family for their support and encouragement, especially my wife Betty for her patience and seemingly endless proofreading, my son Brian for his technical challenges, and his wife Nancy for final proofreading.

CONTENTS

CONTENTS CONTINUED

Foreword
by Dr. Allen Ward

Dr. Ward has become the leading spokesman to call attention to the merits of the principles used by Toyota in product development. While a professor at the University of Michigan, he led a study of Toyota's system and found that how the company goes about developing new products is as important to the company's success as its revered Toyota Production System. The Toyota Product Development System simply has not received the same high level of publicity. Dr. Ward has been applying these principles ever since at such well-known companies as General Motors, Delphi, and Danfoss.

We now live in a post-bubble economy. Many of the companies most admired in the '90s now are in serious trouble. Stock markets in the US and Europe have declined precipitously; trillions of dollars have been lost. Some prominent economists forecast possible worldwide deflation and prolonged recession.

Japan has been in a similar post-bubble economy for a decade. Yet two companies in Japan—Honda and Toyota—posted record profits in 2001. Toyota's are 90% better still for the first half of 2002. Can we learn from them in order to do as well, no matter what happens to the world economy?

We can—but it will be a challenge. Here's an example of how big. When I ask American engineers and engineering managers at Toyota how much of their time they spend "creating value" or "creating knowledge" or "doing engineering" the answer averages about 80%. When I ask American engineers and engineering managers at large US companies the same question, the answers average less than 20%. Mid-size Scandinavian companies average about 40%, almost midway between the two.

Does your common sense tell you that you can achieve a four to one improvement in so fundamental a measurement by doing what you've always done, but rearranging it? Or do you think a more fundamental change will be required?

In fact, Toyota and Honda violate the most basic *conventional assumptions of post-WWII business.* These assumptions can be summarized in The Golden Rule.

"He who has the gold makes the rules."

This rule expands into four assumptions:

1) The "importance of capital" assumption: Capital, labor, and materials are the primary inputs to production, and capital is the most important, the one that controls the others.

2) The "mass production" assumption: We prosper by investing capital to reduce labor requirements and using the power of our capital to squeeze the suppliers of materials.

3) The "scientific management" assumption: Three kinds of people exist in corporations: managers who make decisions and represent the owners of capital; workers who execute the decisions; and experts who define procedures, metrics, and incentives.

4) The "financial management" assumption: the most important business activity is making good financial decisions to invest in areas of growth, particularly by buying "hot" companies, while slashing costs elsewhere.

So how did these assumptions work out in the '90s? Well:

• "He who had the gold" was swiftly relieved of it by smooth talkers with a good story and well-fudged accounts.

• Capital became nearly free. Its investment in the hottest new Internet technologies produced no returns on investment—but enriched a lot of workers.

• Over and over, forceful, charismatic, cost-cutting leadership produced high short-term profits, enthusiastic press — and then disaster. At Ford, for example, Nasser was able to show dramatic profits by partly slashing development costs and times. Predictably, four years later, Ford began having the terrifying recall problems that still haunt it.

• The *majority* of the investment decisions by highly trained, touted, and experienced CEOs led to significant, often dramatic, loss of stockholder value. Clever investments in coming technologies — the Internet and telecommunications — lost *more than a trillion* dollars.

• 10 of the 19 "top Harvard MBA CEOs of 1990" led their companies into disaster.

But Toyota and Honda made different assumptions. They have been developing their implications over decades, and that development is only now fully paying off. They believe:

a) The most important input to production is knowledge.

b) With knowledge, we can reduce the costs and improve the benefits of the costs of labor hours, capital, and materials.

c) Companies have only one kind of employee: everyone creates knowledge and acts on it for the good of the whole.

d) Knowledge cannot be purchased: indeed, mergers normally result in a net loss of knowledge. So we have to create knowledge by learning. Most learning occurs during "product development".

Or to summarize, we have the Knowledge Rule: "Nature and markets make the rules. We profit by learning them."

Armed with these concepts, we can understand why Toyota and Honda have continued to be successful and others have had difficulty despite widespread attempts to implement lean manufacturing and even Lean Thinking. The use of lean concepts is only one factor behind their success.

First, "product development" (broadly understood to include the development of the entire value cycle, from suppliers through plants into products and out to customers) is the real key to success. Many executives were misled by Toyota's forceful insistence that it is a manufacturing company, and its emphasis on reducing waste. Neither emphasis is strong at Honda; both points are really ways of emphasizing the importance of knowledge. Nor are Toyota's and Honda's manufacturing systems very similar. But intellectual investments in development have led Toyota and Honda to nearly identical development systems.

11

These enable Toyota, for example, to introduce about twice as many new vehicles each year as much larger GM, and with "designed-in" quality in 2001 *14 times* as high as Ford's (as measured by recalls).

Second, knowledge must be constructed internally; but scientific management gets in the way.

You cannot effectively buy knowledge, because unless you have it, you can't tell the quality of what you are buying. The "dot-com" technological revolution may be the first in history from which *none* of the pioneering companies will produce positive return on investment. It is also the first led by MBAs rather than technical experts. As a result, huge investments in "high tech" were thrown away because the products didn't actually do anything customers would pay for.

Several business leaders have already tried "Theory Y" or "learning organization" methods to replace scientific management and the "Golden Rule." Most achieved some initial success, followed by long-term failure. This was inevitable. Scientific management is a poor theory, but has been the only fully worked out theory available until now—and we can no more run a large company without management theory than we can build spacecraft without engineering theory.

Toyota has spent 100 years working out the details of how to actually operate a learning organization. I believe we can now present that experience as a coherent and detailed theory, and we have seen dramatic results in companies that have applied it.

This book is an engaging, suspenseful, and humorous introduction to those concepts—one in which you will see many people you know in business, and perhaps even yourself. It points the way to corporate transformation, from the Golden Rule to the Knowledge Rule. Read it, enjoy it, learn from it, and take action.

Introduction
The Magic of Toyota / The Challenge of Change

In 1990, the book *The Machine that Changed the World* introduced the English-speaking world to the power of the Toyota Production System. This continuous-flow method of manufacturing requires significantly less direct labor, virtually eliminates work-in-process and parts inventory, and results in far fewer defects, i.e. much higher quality, than is typically the experience of mass manufacturers. No wonder the Lean Manufacturing Initiative followed, and with it, the objective of spreading lean manufacturing throughout the world.

However, the Toyota Product Development System is every bit as important to the prosperity of Toyota as its production system. Arguably, it has been even more of a factor in helping to maintain the high level of success the company has enjoyed year after year. Until now very little was known about the specifics of the system.

Under the banner of Lean Product Development, efforts have been focused mainly on systematic waste reduction and the application of lean manufacturing techniques to product development. Certainly, the elimination of non-value-added activities and the institution of other lean principles can make a difference. But there is much more to the Toyota system. Lean Product Development by itself can take a company only part of the way toward the efficiency of the Toyota System. The reason is simple. The Toyota Product Development System springs from a totally different paradigm than the one that forms the basis of product development systems used by the vast majority of companies in the western world. This book will explain that paradigm and the great potential it offers.

There is more. This book will explain how the Toyota model

can be implemented. Normally, large-scale changes are very difficult to achieve within a reasonable time frame. Yet a proven methodology does exist.

Understanding the magic of the Toyota Product Development System by itself may be intellectually stimulating, but this by itself will not put a company ahead of the competition. What will do so is understanding how to quickly adapt the system. This is the real magic I wish to convey and the primary objective of this book.

Product Development: A Definition

What is product development? A useful definition is that it is the collective activities, or system, that a company uses to convert its technology and ideas into a stream of products that meet the needs of customers and the strategic goals of the company.

Product Development: Two Decades of Change

In twenty-five years, product development has changed significantly from a rather basic, simple approach (one designer and one slide rule) to an arena filled with great complexity (a structured team equipped with CAD/CAM, Six Sigma analysis, manufacturability experts, defined processes, and extensive metrics). All of this complexity was introduced for good reasons. But that complexity introduces numerous problems, including significant communication breakdowns and the debilitating loss of personal responsibility.

The simple reporting structure of designer to technical manager has become matrixed. This shift may look good at first glance. But often the bureaucracy of committees replaces sound technical leadership.

The quest for quality, starting with Deming and Juran and continuing through Six Sigma, has led to a more structured and rigid development approach. Although the quality movement has given product quality the emphasis it is due, the movement has also overlaid a confusing network of design structure.

The business process reengineering revolution was instrumental in focusing improvement on the work or process, but it also added complex procedural documentation. And certainly, design automation has added extensive design and analysis capability, as well as complexity, to the process. These changes may seem positive, but they make the product development process more complicated than ever. This trend continues as additional features are added in the attempt to achieve continuous improvement.

Is all of this added complexity and structure bad, or is it just a necessary result of the evolving and improving product development processes? In the computer world, there is no doubt that the Windows shell has made the underlying DOS operating system much more user friendly, but it has done so at the price of complexity, speed, and reliability. So the question is: Are the layers of product development improvements over the years the answer, or are they a veneer that masks fundamental flaws in the operational foundation?

The Report Card

Over the past two decades product development has improved dramatically in two important areas—quality and manufacturing compatibility. There's no doubt that current design capabilities, in terms of expected product quality, reliability, and ease of manufacturing, are superior across all manufacturing companies. The overall report card on improvement is positive.

But there is a dark side:

• American value-added productivity, i.e. creating useful knowledge for the end-user, is reported as ~20% for engineers; ~5% for managers.

• The transfer of technical knowledge across projects is generally low.

• High variances in performance exist between best and worst programs.

• Projects are rarely completed per their original schedules.

• Overhead rates are continually increasing, reflecting increasing system complexity.

• The design experience level of the engineering staff is decreasing as more engineers move quickly into administrative management. The average design engineer sees very few complete design cycles.

Here is the bottom line report: Product development has made solid progress in several important areas, but it has done so at a high price in others. Unless the underlying system is challenged, the ability to achieve gains in the future must be questioned. But there is another way.

The Magic of Toyota

Let's look at Toyota:

• Toyota engineers and managers normally achieve ~80% value-added productivity. This is ~4X the typical American manufacturer.

• From every perspective—customer feedback, lack of manufacturing problems, and level of product recalls—Toyota is recognized as offering the highest quality in the industry.

• Toyota never misses its milestone dates.

• Toyota has highly consistent and profitable programs.

• Toyota has highly experienced design engineers with many design cycles completed.

• Toyota has very little dependence on typical American initiatives of controlled complexity: design automation, Six Sigma, Concurrent Engineering, co-location.

A comparison of the differences between development performance at Toyota and that of the typical manufacturer is truly remarkable. It is highly improbable, for example, that a company with 20%, or even 40%, productivity will ever be able to compete successfully with a company operating at 80%. How this difference is achieved requires a deep and thorough examination of the fundamental operational philosophies of the Toyota

Product Development System and that used by others.

If a typical American company is able to transform itself to Toyota level performance, what benefits can be expected? The results would be astounding:

- 4X increase in development productivity
- 2-3X decrease in development cycle time
- 2-3X decrease in development cost
- 2-10X increase in innovation
- 2-5X decrease in development risk

The Challenge

Emulating Toyota would be simple if it were only necessary to compare processes, define the differences, and rearrange activities to conform to the Toyota model. Unfortunately, it isn't that easy. Toyota's system isn't just different. What drives Toyota's success is a totally different operating philosophy. The cold truth is, matching the level of productivity achieved by Toyota cannot be accomplished strictly by copying techniques. First, it is necessary to understand thoroughly the underpinnings of Toyota's development system. Only then will it be possible to adapt these to your company and industry.

The Approach

What will it take? A fundamental paradigm shift in how your company approaches product development. Experience indicates this won't be easy. It's human nature to resist change. Yet management will have to change its thinking and adopt a brand new philosophy concerning product development.

Each chapter of this book builds on the previous one, as a case study unfolds, to communicate how this shift can occur. Each chapter is followed by discussion. My objective is to reveal the new way of thinking required in a way that will become increasingly clear as you turn the pages. In doing so, my hope is that you will come to agree that knowledge and effective learning form the correct foundation for both successful product development and successful change.

This book is about the interaction of people and how to manage or influence that interaction. Over the years, I've worked with many companies where I've observed relationships between people that mirror themselves in their individual goals, conflicts, and reactions to change. I suspect that most readers will recognize the human dynamics in the storyline, and they will understand how these dynamics result in the success or failure of major company initiatives. I hope that by interweaving the technical and people stories, I will convey the difficulties and the opportunities for change.

I hope you enjoy this journey into a new way of thinking.

Chapter 1

Opportunity and Denial
(The Power of Bureaucracy)

How many opportunities for improvement are ignored because we don't recognize the opportunity. Or we recognize the opportunity, but ignore it for fear of upsetting the status quo of the organization.

Wednesday morning, Infrared Technologies Corporation, Process Steering & Control Team Meeting

I didn't actually witness the scene that follows, but I heard about it. It happened at a meeting that began at 8 o'clock sharp on a Wednesday morning. The place was a sparse conference room located near the front entrance of the Infrared Technologies Corporation building with a large window running along one wall and overlooking the parking lot—though you wouldn't know it because the Venetian blinds were closed.

The team leader opened the meeting with a hearty, "Good morning." His name was Doyle Mattingly. He glanced from one attendee to another as they sleepily acknowledged him. He told them that the purpose of the meeting was to review proposed changes or issues with the standard product development process, PDSP (Product Development Standard Process). Our man Doyle had led the development of the standard process over the last several years. Besides him, six other process experts were on the team. When not attending meetings like this, their primary jobs were training. They also administered the standard process.

The room set up, a typical IRT meeting room, consisted of a single table seating 10 or so people and a few chairs around the periphery of the room. Today's attendance included several other people who would either be presenting or listening. Doyle placed a slide of the agenda on the viewgraph and continued, "We have three presenters today. Then we have several open items from last month. Hopefully, we'll be out of here by ten."

In a slightly sarcastic tone, one of the steering team said, "AM or PM?"

"I believe it will be AM, today, Sam," Doyle said. He forced a smile. "Our first presenter is Jan Morris, a design engineer within the Military Projects department. Jan?"

Jan stood, nodded and walked to the front of the room. Dressed in a dark blue jacket and skirt and a white blouse, she cut a trim figure. A mechanical engineer who'd hired into IRT seven years earlier after graduating from Arizona State, she loved design. In fact, she already had one patent on an IR cooler assembly, and was respected for her design and analysis capabilities.

A voice came from the back of the room. "Before Jan starts, let me say a couple of words. I'm Vijay Suran, the program manager on the ASN50 project. Jan works for me and has been involved part time with a consortium project for the last year. I asked her to report here because there's some very interesting process-related information coming out of the project."

Doyle said, "Hi, Vijay. Haven't seen you in a while. How've you been?" He turned immediately to the front of the room.

Jan cleared her throat and stood poised. "Good Morning. The consortium I'm working with is a project within NCMS, the National Center for Manufacturing Sciences. The companies represented include car companies and their suppliers, some defense companies, and a few other smaller companies. Our project goal is to investigate the product development processes of highly successful companies and to find new paradigms that can be adapted back at our individual companies. We've focused on breakthrough concepts as opposed to 'best practice' process improvements."

Doyle looked concerned. "Jan, you didn't give those companies access to our PDSP process, did you? We consider that proprietary."

Jan pursed her lips, then said, "They looked at it, but I didn't give out copies. The truth is, no one seemed that interested. In fact, they all had similar looking documentation. All the other companies represented use an approach that boils down to detailed procedural documentation to control product development—like ours."

Clearly, Doyle wasn't happy. "The processes might have looked the same, but ours is loaded with recognized best practices. Please be careful with the process."

Jan shrugged and continued, "After studying a lot of companies, the only approach we found to be truly unique was Toyota's development methodology. As everyone knows, there's a lot of information on Toyota's lean manufacturing process. But, very little is known about their product development. Today I want to briefly outline their environment. I think this is going to pique your interest. I've many more details that can be covered at a later date. Vijay thought this committee was a place to start disseminating this information."

Jan glanced around the room and then continued. "Toyota is renowned for the quality of its products, but many don't realize it also has a development cycle time that's about half that of its competitors'. One result is, the company makes more profit per car than any automaker. Our project estimated their productivity at about four times the U.S. Big Three. They develop products using an entirely different methodology from ours. Let me walk you through some of the highlights."

Glancing down at notes, Jan read the points, pausing briefly after each.

"Toyota does not have a detailed step-by-step process describing how to do development. They have a simple project plan that highlights key dates and responsibilities.

"Toyota applies tremendous rigor to how they capture

learning. They study both what works and what doesn't work, and they systemically document and disseminate the information. They perform extensive prototyping at the subsystem level and they heavily utilize trade curves for analyzing performance. Everyone has ready access to the knowledge and everyone is expected to use it, including management.

"For example, Toyota does not set hard specifications at the start of a project, but establishes performance, physical size, and cost targets that mature along with the design.

"For each vehicle program, Toyota does not establish an early system level design, but instead establishes sets of possibilities for each subsystem, many of which are carried far into the design process. These sets consider all functional and manufacturing perspectives, building redundancy to risk while maintaining design flexibility. The final system design is developed through systematic combining and narrowing of these sets."

She took a breath and looked around the room to mostly blank stares. With a slight shake of her head, she said, "The Toyota development system can be considered more an iterative process, a spiral with a continuing elimination, addition, and combination of possibilities.

"What's the bottom line on Toyota's brilliant approach? What they have is really an overall development environment rather than a process in the traditional sense. New products more or less are allowed to emerge from the collective learning at the subsystem level. This operational philosophy obviously has a dramatic impact on leadership styles, design reviews, personnel development, project planning, and more."

Jan's enthusiasm showed through in the tone of her voice and her pacing. "Toyota's results are astounding. They develop cars with the highest quality, with four times the productivity, in half the time, with more innovation, and with less risk than the big three U.S. automakers. They make more profits consistently, even in the depressed Japanese economy."

She put down her notes. "I believe that the Toyota system is a fundamentally superior development environment to our traditional process. I'd like to ask for your help to better understand the implications and the potential for IRT. Our group at NCMS has worked out many of the organizational changes required to adapt Toyota's environment to our culture. I'd be glad to share that information when appropriate. Thank you for your time." Jan smiled and waited for feedback, fully expecting interest and questions.

Slowly, Doyle surveyed the room, wearing a frown that surely discouraged any comments from his committee. He then turned to Jan, pausing perhaps to frame his thoughts. Carefully, he began. "Jan, you seem to be suggesting that we revisit many of the fundamental precepts of our PDSP process based on the results of your NCMS project, correct?"

No doubt surprised by this reaction, Jan said, "I'm not really suggesting that. My presentation is only a brief overview of a lot of information our project uncovered and analyzed by studying Toyota and other companies. I'm just trying to open a dialog with the process experts in the company to apply what makes sense."

Doyle continued in a patronizing tone. "We don't make cars, Jan. We make high tech devices primarily for the military. The nature of our business requires detailed processes and we've spent many years optimizing our PDSP process. I can't imagine we could learn anything from a car company. This simply doesn't apply to our business."

An incredulous look appeared on Jan's face.

Vijay stepped in. "Doyle, almost all of our products have a detector assembly, a power supply assembly, an optics layout, and a computer assembly. Why is that any different from vehicle design when it comes to a development environment? Their principles will work here as well as they would on any system design in any industry."

Obviously annoyed, Doyle said, "Irrelevant. Besides that, I

don't see the process. The PDSP is and will continue to be our process. Jan, if you can identify and recommend some specific changes, then we'll listen. Our process clearly defines recognized best practices and the timeline for executing them. This structure is really critical to maintaining our development schedules. Anything less appears confusing at best, and chaotic at worst." Doyle stared at her. "Anything else?"

Jan's brow was furrowed. "I'm sorry. I guess I must not have done a good job of explaining. Toyota's development environment is one in which all research and all knowledge gained from failures and successes from all previous projects are readily available and accessible. This knowledge is expected to be applied to new products. That's a powerful organizational basis for development. On the other hand, our PDSP is a series of process steps that look good on paper. But it offers the illusion of control to administrators while promoting product development as a series of individual projects rather than an integrated learning environment. Do you really not see, or appreciate, the difference?"

She took a breath and continued. "And what do we do with results? Lessons-learned from our prior projects are systemically buried in personal files. Our projects are always behind schedule and over cost. Even our beloved schedule charts, that always look good at the start of a project, are non-existent at the end. Our engineers continually waste time looking for information that should be easily accessible, or preparing and attending useless meetings to satisfy administrative requirements. And what's the impact on manufacturing? I worked extensively on the assembly floor last year and can tell you the problems coming out of product development were confusing at best and chaotic at worse. I have no idea how you can call that best practice, except maybe from a bureaucratic perspective. In fact, are you aware that many of our best engineers consider the PDSP a joke? Yet, somehow, management believes that it's such a success that even meaningful alternatives from highly successful companies are not worthy of any investigation."

Jan looked straight at Doyle and slapped her side. "Thank you for your interest and encouragement. I think it's best for me to leave now."

All that could be heard was a truck accelerating through gears on the highway half a mile away as Jan headed for the exit. Vijay followed close behind.

Vijay hurried to catch up. "Jan, hold up."

She turned, her face flushed and her eyes glistening with tears. "Oh, Vijay. I-I really don't want to talk now. I know you didn't expect that any more than I did, but you know how much that says about this company when a man like that and his puppet committee are put in charge of our product development processes. It says this company values administrative bureaucracy more than engineering excellence. I've got to tell you, I've been looking outside and have an offer from a small company that I've been thinking about."

Vijay stood before Jan, speechless, as she took a breath. "I really appreciate the training you gave me, Vijay. And I appreciate your support. I don't want to put you in a bind, but at this point, I don't see how I can stay."

"Don't do anything rash," was all Vijay could muster.

"I will sleep on it, okay? My husband and I like this town. We aren't crazy about the idea of relocating. Tell you what. I've got some vacation days coming up. That will give me time to think"

Vijay said, "Take the time you need. I want you to stay, Jan. I'll do whatever it takes to keep you here." He paused. "But, of course, I understand how you feel."

Jan walked through security.

Vijay mumbled, "Damn you, Doyle. What has this company become?"

DISCUSSION

So, what just happened? Jan had a confrontation with someone who worked in a totally different paradigm than what she described as existing at Toyota. That person's career was dependent not on the success of the company, but on the success of his paradigm. Unfortunately, this dichotomy is probably more the norm than the exception at most companies. A while back, I was consulting in another country with an automotive supplier. We were developing a pilot project using many of the Toyota concepts. The process czar, a Detroit manager, attended one of the meetings. His primary goal was to protect the sanctity of the standard process. He called me aside, introduced himself, and made sure I understood the limitations of the pilot relative to the overall process. Although the pilot had been chartered based on some visionary thought of a mid-level manager, the czar made sure the effort remained contained. With no management support or encouragement, the pilot simply faded over time.

The process of product development, particularly when based on methods practiced by large manufacturing companies, has become a bastion of the command and control paradigm. Layers of administration, detailed task-based planning systems, and formal design reviews all contribute to maintenance of organizational status quo. Bureaucracies, which have grown bloated over the years, shield themselves from major philosophical changes.

To understand the level of change suggested by this book, let's examine one example of the Toyota type development environment. Consider a commercial winery. A management staff runs the finances. Functional organizations take care of barrels, bottles, harvesting, and marketing. There are suppliers—grape farmers, cork and bottle manufacturers, label makers—and there is also a winemaker who is the chief engineer. No one actually works for the winemaker, but it is his or her wine. Mother Nature sets the harvest schedule. Firm dates exist for crushing, racking, bottling, and key wine shows. These dates are *always* met. The winemaker makes decisions on which grapes go to the reserve brand for the wine connoisseur, which to the winery brand, and which are blended for the bulk wine. Everyone in the process is experienced, learning more and better techniques each year. An individual's performance is measured strictly on his or her value to the process. A good winemaker will carefully oversee all parts of the process by direct observation, not with administrative reviews. In summary, there are no formal reviews. There are no committees. There are no schedule slippages. However, expertise exists at every level. There are clear personnel responsibilities. And the winemaker is the best engineer, with the most technical knowledge of the product, the customer, and of the overall process.

The simple snapshot above of how product development is carried out in the wine industry suggests a rich environment both in capability and potential. The process is not based on structure and control, but on expertise and product emergence. The chasm is huge between this way of working and established product development bureaucracies. To cross this chasm, it will be critical to identify, adapt and support the organizational underpinnings of this environment. This is the primary focus of this book.

Our challenges before us are to understand the foundation of the Toyota development system, to adapt it to a different culture, and then to actually make the transition.

The IRT case study thus far seems to have come to an end. The standard process remains unscathed and in firm bureaucratic control. The young engineer has other employment beckoning that can satisfy her goals and her desire to spread her technological wings. Unfortunately, this is an ongoing scenario today in many companies. Does it have to remain so? Perhaps yes, perhaps no. If a change in organizational thinking is to occur, it's very likely that some sort of disruption in management will have to precede it.

Let's return to IRT Corporation.

Chapter 2

A Call to Action
(The Power of Engaged Leadership)

Every change must be accompanied by a valid case for action and an engaged leader. Without both, change efforts eventually tend to just fade away.

Monday morning, Infrared Technologies Corporation

Donna, our group secretary, was at her desk, half hidden by a computer monitor. She raised her head when I walked in and looked at me with big doe eyes. A tiny smirk appeared. "Good morning, Jon. So glad you could make it in this morning."

It was only 8:30, but a similar wisecrack had come whizzing at me practically every day since I'd given my notice to retire. Actually, after so many years of arriving by 6:30, I did feel a little guilty about my tardiness.

With retirement in sight, offering up lighthearted banter had become a chore. Nevertheless, I gave it a go. "Gee thanks, Donna. It was a struggle, but I needed to get in before the coffee break."

"As a matter of fact, Troy called and asked you to meet him in the cafeteria for breakfast. But you do have the 9 a.m. strategic manufacturing planning meeting. You're not going to miss another one, are you?"

She wouldn't seem to accept that I never liked that stupid meeting. I damn sure didn't have to deal with it now. In fact, as the retiring senior technologist, my presence was more disruptive than helpful. Besides, I had some serious desk cleaning to do.

"Oh, I'll probably go in late. Don't want Troy to have to eat by himself. Wouldn't be fair of me."

Donna smiled that smirky smile as I headed out, feet dragging all the way. I knew I should attend that meeting, but I'd lost interest. I'd suffered through so many meetings in which clear and logical decision-making had been replaced by the endless and ongoing chatter of strategic committees. Mostly they didn't make decisions. At least not many that made sense. Information swirled and confusion reigned. Yep, it was definitely time for me to leave.

My thoughts rambled along such lines as I strolled to the cafeteria. Hard to believe that after 31 years I had only three weeks until retirement. Never thought I'd retire at 55. I'd wanted to be the only manufacturing technologist to ever become a Principal Fellow. Would have made it, too, probably next year. Oh well, having made Senior Fellow wasn't bad. Heck, there were only four in the company, and only one in my area of manufacturing.

I trudged along. The cafeteria doorway came into view. Why did I feel so blah? Discouragement, perhaps. It was hard to believe that we'd slipped so far in market share with our great production facilities and the highest quality in our business. Yeah, we were lean and mean in manufacturing, but we just couldn't seem to get the right product out at the right time.

Ah, forget it. Take the retirement package and run.

I came through the door and saw Troy—already in the cafeteria as usual. He wasn't even making an attempt to act busy. We'd worked together for 20 years and had made a pretty darn good team. They called us the manufacturing mafia. With Troy as the manufacturing planning manager, we took a sort of perverse pleasure in being a thorn in the side of so many engineers in product development.

There'd always been conflict between design engineering and manufacturing. Each identified the other as the problem. What a battle of wills.

I just got coffee. Troy had his morning sweet roll. He'd put on about 10 pounds since we both announced retirement.

"So Troy," I said. "What's your schedule today? I assume you're going to the SPM meeting at 9."

"Yeah, right," he replied sarcastically, as he devoured the last bite of roll. "Actually, I have a 1:30 tee time." He looked straight at me. "You on? It's supposed to get cold tomorrow."

Yesterday I'd sworn I'd spend the day responding to a long list of emails that had been accumulating.

"Sure," I said. "Why not?" The emails could wait. "I'll meet you there."

His day now set, Troy switched to his morning gripe session. "Can you believe we lost the tank sight contract to Raytheon? We invented that business. They said we were too expensive, too late, and too heavy. Watch Jorgenson blame manufacturing. The idiot insisted the Army really wanted all that technology."

Nathan Jorgenson was the Military Products manager, an infrared technology zealot, a fact demonstrated throughout the product line.

I joined in. "Uh-huh, and Ford announced it was going to delay adding the infrared sensor to the next generation Lincoln. They couldn't wait on our timetable for the new prototype. Said it'd put them behind on next year's planning. I can't believe we've let that market slide so long."

Troy shrugged. "Heck, I'm not complaining. The pressure to reduce staff around here ended up in a nice package for us." He'd been itching to retire for years. "Now, let's get serious. How many strokes you gonna give me?"

That conversation got me thinking about the company's milestones. I reviewed them in my mind as I walked back to my office. We didn't invent infrared technology, but we sure could develop applications that the DoD wanted, and we could do it fast and cheap. We had all the patents on low cost detectors and cooling technologies. We won the National Quality Award. We were selected by Ford to deploy the technologies in automobiles, and we had a working model for home security applications. What had gone wrong? I didn't like to think about it, but for me, early retirement seemed like a personal failure. This company had been my home for so long, and now . . .

Donna just smiled as I walked into my office. I sat down and hit the space bar on the keyboard. Fifty new messages filled the screen. Oh well, it gave me something to do.

A minute later, Donna appeared in my doorway holding up a pink phone message slip. "Jack Holder called. He wants you to call him."

I hadn't talked to Jack since I'd announced my retirement, but I'd halfway expected him to try to talk me out of it. As executive production operations vice president, Jack had been my mentor. He was the only top level manager who had his act together. Early on, he'd assigned me as his primary troubleshooter, and later, was largely responsible for my election as Senior Fellow. I assumed he was calling to wish me well in retirement.

I punched in his extension. "Hi Ann, this is Jon Stevens. I'm returning Jack's call."

"Hi, Jon. He's been expecting you. Hang on."

Except for Donna, Ann had always been my favorite secretary. She'd never acquired that air of superiority as she moved up with Jack.

In a few moments, Jack came on. He spent the first minute or two giving me a hard time about being too young to retire. This actually put me at ease. He didn't seem disappointed. Then he asked whether I could attend a meeting at 2 p.m. Bummer. But I decided not to say that he was screwing up my golf game.

"Sure," I said. I felt a tiny wave of apprehension, but also excitement. "What's it about?" As a Senior Fellow, maybe it was a special going away party.

"No time to go into details now, Jon. I'll see you there, okay?"

After I hung up, I picked up the receiver and punched in another extension. "Troy, old buddy, about our golf date . . . "

I arrived for the meeting 10 minutes early and decided to take a chair near the back. My plan was to stay somewhat inconspicuous, and I was hoping to get a quick word with Jack. I really didn't like being at a meeting when I was totally unaware of the agenda. Jack was there already, but in a private discussion with Grant Loving, the executive VP over all program operations. 'Teflon' Grant somehow never seemed to get personal blame for the dismal performance of his projects. Maybe it was because of the image he projected. He was tall, good looking, articulate—quite a contrast to Jack, who was short, wiry, outspoken, had a flattop even though he was balding.

I could tell this wasn't going to be a surprise retirement party, and I was starting to become uneasy. This room was the typical large room setup: a long oval table seating 10 to 15, and an outer circle of about 30 chairs around the periphery. It always amused me how, by some unwritten pecking order, everybody knew where to sit. Each person always took his or her position based on where the highest-ranking person positioned himself. Jack always took the left front chair. Grant always took the middle back, which always seemed weird since he had to see through the viewgraph machine. I noticed that today Grant was sitting in the second chair up front next to Jack. This was really strange.

Across the table, Grant's administrator fiddled with some papers, then put up the agenda slide (Figure 2a) and focused the viewgraph.

Damn. This was a stupid quarterly program review. What the hell was Jack doing here? What the hell was I doing here?

My uneasiness grew as the room slowly filled. The VP's over each of the business segments and functional organizations filed in and sat down at the oval table. Jack's presence seemed to disrupt their normal routine. It was amusing to see some confusion on the part of most of them concerning where, exactly, to sit. Kind of fun to watch, actually. Several acknowledged my attendance. I was sure they were wondering what the hell I was doing here, in their org meeting. I agreed.

Second Quarter Program Review
- Agenda -

Opening Comments	Grant Loving	2:00
Military Products	Nathan Jorgenson	2:20
Automotive Products	Charles Osgood	2:40
Civilian Avionics	Wayne Tillotson	3:00
Security Systems	Christine Dumas	3:20
PSI Process Deployment	Doyle Mattingly	3:40
Engineering Operations	Jim Shipmann	4:00
Summary	Grant Loving	4:20

(Figure 2a)

The room was definitely tense. The engineering guys had a good ol' boy club atmosphere. I'm sure Jack's presence was somewhat disconcerting. It amazed me how many people were filling up the room periphery. Most I didn't know, but I assumed they were there as support to their managers.

Finally, a friendly face showed up. Greg Drucker was a senior member on our technical promotion ladder who had worked many years for me as staff expert on Six Sigma after we implemented it in manufacturing. Reluctantly, I'd let him move into engineering to head up a cost improvement team in the effort to deploy concurrent engineering. He was a great engineer. I 'd often wished I still had him. He saw me, waved, came over and sat down.

"What are you doing here, short timer?"

"Afraid I haven't got a clue."

Greg looked to the front. "Whoa! What's Jack doing here? What's going on?"

"Damned if I know. Anyway, what are you doing here? I thought you were leading a critical cost analysis on one of our many screwed up, over-budget projects."

Greg responded that he always prepared the project cost status for Jim Shipmann, the VP for Engineering Services. He shrugged when I commented on the lost productivity caused by wasting his time in a meeting like this.

At about ten after two, Grant's administrator threw the agenda foil up on the projector, and announced that Grant would say a few words to start the meeting. Things were getting interesting. I was hoping he was going to apologize for screwing up the company, but he started by discussing his long-term interest in new technology and how the company had to do a better job of leveraging its broad technology base in infrared technology.

Or maybe getting actual products out the door at reasonable costs, I thought.

Then he announced he was going to head up a special task force to organize and enhance our technology backbone. Grinning inwardly, it was apparent to me he was being sent into exile under the pretext of a special assignment.

Then came the shocker. He announced that Jack—mean old manufacturing Jack—was going to head up Engineering. This was really going to break up the engineering good ol' boy promotion scheme. Hallelujah! I shouted inwardly.

But my shock was nothing compared to the deer-in-headlights look on the faces of the managers around the table. It was nothing less than total fear.

Grant thanked everyone for their support and said he was sure Jack would get the same cooperation.

Jack would see to that, I thought. This meeting was more fun than golf. I was hoping Jack had invited me just for the enjoyment of it. Grant excused himself and left, presumably to get on with his new challenge. Actually, Jack had probably insisted he get the hell out after his farewell speech.

The room was so quiet I could hear myself breathe. Jack slowly stood. This was a very scary man. He'd started with the company as a machinist directly out of the Marines, had obtained his mechanical engineering degree at night and worked his way up through the manufacturing engineering ranks. Jack had been executive VP over production for five years now. He'd won numerous awards for his automation of the inventory management of our manufacturing facilities. Then he'd had the guts to scrap it all when the just-in-time, lean philosophy appeared. In fact, most agreed the manufacturing efficiency achieved through his early adoption of lean had been what drove us to the top of the military market and opened markets in the auto and consumer segments. *If only we had delivered the products.*

I'd come over from engineering to help Jack solve automation software problems 15 years ago. As a Senior Fellow now, I still worked primarily on the issues he was concerned with. Because of his temper, though, he was widely feared across the company. But he was also respected as a straight shooter.

Jack surveyed the room. He started to speak, slowly at first. "You all know me as just an old manufacturing guy, and you're probably wondering why I was selected for this job. Well, I guess we'll just have to figure it out together. You all know our company's facing some big challenges. Our profits are deteriorating. Our market share is shrinking. Our overhead rate is growing. I'm very interested to hear your views today. I promise I'll listen. But let me say one thing right now. We must change if we're going to meet the goals of the company. I'm hoping each of you will lead the way." Jack nodded, and the administrator put the agenda chart back up.

Each manager had 20 minutes to review where they stood in relation to their goals and their plans. The business segment managers were to focus on business issues, while the functional line managers were to focus on strategy or initiative issues. This format had been standard for as long as I could remember.

First up was Nathan Jorgenson, who'd been responsible for the Military Products Division for years. This used to be our only business, and at one time we had 70% of the market. Under his watch, we were now third with about 15% share. While the quality of our output was still the best in the business, our unit cost and responsiveness to deployment speed had cost us dearly. In addition, our overhead rate was 20% higher than our competitors. It never made sense to me how Nathan kept his position.

Thirty-five minutes later, Nathan finished his presentation. It was, in short, a boring laundry list of misses—one project was late because of one supplier, another because of a major computer problem, and another because of slow drafting and CAD database problems. Several projects were on schedule based on drawing count completion. Everybody in the room knew that his drawing count included trivial drawings, a gentlemen's agreement to believe everybody's exaggerations. He'd also done three audits to find how well his people were following the standard product development process. Their compliance was improving. This metric had elicited an enthusiastic "attaboy" from Doyle Mattingly, the leader of the team that had spent five mil so far on developing a standard process for everyone to follow.

During Nathan's presentation, I did see some eyes rolling from the young people around the room. Maybe there was still hope for the future of this company.

One by one, each manager masterfully painted a rosy picture of an obviously failing business. I was impressed with their smoothness, a trait that was always missing in my repertoire. It was a damn good thing IRT had a technical promotion ladder for me to follow.

Jack was amazingly quiet during the presentations. Not one stayed on schedule. Two had misspelled words. Maybe the job itself caused great managers to go soft. I did enjoy it when Jack asked Charles Osgood, manager of Automotive Products Segment, whether he really thought the average Ford owner truly cared that our system could withstand a sidewinder missile hit. Everybody laughed—except Jack—although I did notice a couple of guys on the back row giving each other a thumbs-up on that comment. It was then 6:30 p.m. in a meeting that was supposed to have ended at five. Luckily, I'd called home at break.

Jack walked slowly to the front of the room. My uneasiness returned.

Why the hell had he invited me to the meeting?

The administrator put up a chart that showed metrics on our standard PDSP process compliance, on Six Sigma metrics, and on CAD deployment; all showed positive trends. Jack didn't say a word, but good ol' Doyle commented on how many of the metrics mirrored the increasing compliance to the standard process. Jack glared at Doyle. Then he nodded to the administrator to put up the next slide.

The administrator put up a second chart (Figure 2b) that

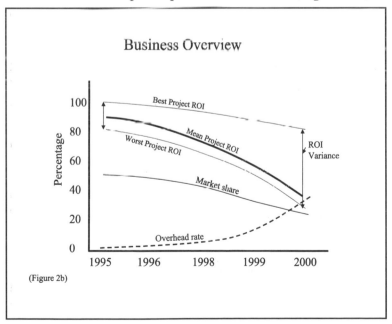

(Figure 2b)

showed our falling market share, our ROI project performance, and our growing overhead rate. Personally, I knew we'd slipped, but these curves were sobering. I was surprised by the growing variances on ROI performance between projects. Jack said nothing but left the chart up for what seemed like an eternity. The numbers were a clear departure from the previous positive chart.

Jack said, "Ladies and Gentlemen, am I the only one who sees a problem here?" Jack looked from one manager to the next.

I noticed Doyle kept his mouth shut. He was no dummy.

Jack continued, "Somehow, we've lost our focus. We've taken our eyes off what's important. Our goal is to make profits—good, solid profits. And that's done by making our customers happy. Happy, satisfied customers mean profits, gentlemen. Do these numbers show profits? Do they show ecstatic customers?"

He paused again, and again he made eye contact with each manager. "We have to change, and we have to change now. I must admit I don't know what to do at this point. I was hoping to get some insight today, but it appears that either you also don't know, or you don't believe you have the right to speak. We have one year to change the direction on this chart." He paused again. "Anybody got an idea where we start?"

I was sure everyone—me included—just wanted out.

By then I was thinking Jack had forgotten I was there. He hadn't acknowledged my presence. But now he turned and stared directly at me. "We need a fresh look at our entire product development operation. You all know or have heard of Jon Stevens, one of our four senior fellows." He pointed at me and I nodded back. If I'd been standing, I think my knees would have buckled. "Jon is taking the early retirement package but still has a few weeks before he leaves. He has a background in engineering and has been a driving force for change within our manufacturing operations. I want him to assemble a team and report back to us in one week with a plan to reverse this trend. I expect everybody here to support him in this effort."

Then he announced he was late for an appointment and had to leave. On his way out, he commented to his administrator,

"Don, please make sure everybody has a spell checker and knows how to use it, and bring a timer to the next meeting." You could have heard a hoot owl call ten miles away as he strode to the door. Then he paused and asked me to meet him in his office at 7 a.m. I nodded and he left.

Oh, brother, it wasn't like Jack to surprise me. Why hadn't he given me some warning? From being a fly on the wall, I'd now become the focus of the meeting. Everyone was waiting for me to say something—as if I had some sort of plan—and somehow I didn't think, "Oh, I'm retiring," would be appropriate.

I stood and muttered something to the effect that since I'd just been brought on today, I needed to talk with Jack and would announce a plan by email tomorrow. To sound authoritative, I asked Don if he could pass a form around to get the attendance at the meeting and contact information. I then asked Greg to leave with me, and we got the heck out of there.

Outside the room, I asked Greg if he could break free for a couple of weeks. I needed some help.

"Sure," he said. "This is going to be fun."

"Can you be at my office at eight tomorrow?" I asked.

"You bet," he said, and he headed back toward his office.

I decided to go straight to the parking lot. It would be a long ride home. The first priority was to shift out of retirement mode.

The strangest feeling came over me as I headed for the mountains: one of remorse and elation all at once.

DISCUSSION

There can be no doubt that a strong, committed leader with a clear vision can change a company. The success of the change will depend on the accuracy of the vision, but the company will change. Henry Ford is the classic example, a strong visionary leader. He was committed. He had a dream of an affordable automobile for all Americans.

Unfortunately, very few Henry Fords exist.

The dilemma faced by IRT is somewhat typical. A company is in trouble, experiencing bad financials and declining performance, but no clear vision exists of what they should be doing differently. Current improvement initiatives offer promises of dramatic improvements, but it's clearly wishful thinking to believe these will really resolve the problems. The promises of improvement that such initiatives hold out keep people moving ahead like lemmings headed for the cliff. Often, employees' resistance to change is cited as the reason for slow adoption of new practices and the subsequent lack of success. Rarely does anyone seriously question the fundamental premise of an initiative. Wishful thinking is the norm.

I have found that change initiatives follow a predictable pattern. Most large companies maintain ongoing quality initiatives. Often, these started with Juran and Crosby training, and they continued through Total Quality Management (TQM) methodologies. Now they're more than likely focused on Six Sigma philosophies. These initiatives usually are accompanied by organizational changes that are made to define and implement the desired quality culture.

Most large companies also use elaborate design automation strategies for engineering efficiency and management of product data. These include a supporting organizational structure for defining and implementing the strategy. In the '90s, Business Process Reengineering became the methodology for major change. This focused on redefining internal company processes for maximum efficiency and value to the customer. This also required organizational structure to support the change methodology. In other words, the desired change required significant organizational structure to implement and sustain it, requiring even more bureaucracy. The question is whether these initiatives, often inspired by external experts, are causing what seems to be a growing quagmire of bureaucracy in American manufacturing, or whether the administrative hierarchy they create is actually self-perpetuating. Regardless, the result is that these experts continually advance these types of improvement initiatives, which may actually discourage the ingenuity that normally would arise from within to resolve issues as they occur.

Although the premise behind these and other improvement initiatives is valuable, the result is that they often lull company leadership with a false sense of security. Management ceases to look for new operational paradigms that might achieve or exceed their goals as they wait for current initiatives to succeed. It is difficult, particularly for leaders with an administrative focus, to challenge existing visions that are well supported by internal organizations and external publications. For these reasons, today's business leaders find it hard to commit to a new paradigm for product development. Nevertheless, that is what's required, regardless of the impact on existing initiatives.

The IRT story reveals strong organizational support to maintain status quo. In fact, administrative careers have been created to support the current operations and improvement methodologies. Many people have a lot to lose if a new operational vision comes to be.

A couple of years ago, while on a consulting visit to an automotive supplier, I was firmly reminded by the company process czar that the company already had a process vision and not to mess with it. In reality, the company didn't have a process vision. The czar had the vision, political savvy, and a job to protect. Company leadership just went along with it.

Luckily, in our case history, IRT's new leader, Jack Holder, is not a proponent of current engineering initiatives. He is also not the typical administrative leader. A visionary, he had already transformed the company into a lean manufacturer. But Jack has no vision for product development. In fact, he believes that engineering should look like manufacturing, a dangerous assumption, but logical based on his background. And so he organizes a team to create a change plan. What he wants is for Jon to create a plan to make the engineering departments as efficient as Jack's manufacturing operations. But what he needs is for Jon to create a new product development paradigm as the vision that can transform the company.

Chapter 3

Establishing the Baseline
(The Power of Assessment)

The root issues must be understood from two perspectives: what is causing them, and what stands between how things should be and what they are. Failure to understand will result in widespread wishful thinking and superficial solutions.

Tuesday morning, Infrared Technologies Corporation

I'd always enjoyed the drive to work, an easy jaunt of about thirty minutes from northwest of Denver to the plant. Drive time allowed me to plan for the day ahead, and to debrief myself on the way home. In fact, some of my best presentations were built in the car. But since the announcement of my retirement, the drive seemed longer. This morning, though, it seemed too short. Or maybe the plan I needed to work out was too big. I'd always had success in leading problem-solving teams, but never this big or in this short an amount of time. Besides, although I prided myself on being able to separate the wheat from the chaff, until now all my projects had been manufacturing-based. This was different. I hadn't worked in product development for 15 years. The principles were the same, but . . . let's say, I just wasn't at all comfortable. What the hell was Jack thinking?

Pulling into the parking lot, I guessed I'd soon find out.

Jack's office was in the "Gray Box," a large, square, dull gray room with offices around the outside and administrative assistants in a smaller interior open area. All the manufacturing VP's were logically arranged around the room. Principal Fellows also got to be in the box. I sometimes wondered whether my goal for achieving that technical rank was just to get a spot. Funny, the engineering head shed, the "mahogany box," was the same but was all wood paneled. Visiting customers were always the rationale for the difference in standard.

Good, Jack was already in.

I saw he was standing behind his big mahogany desk looking at some papers, dressed uncustomarily in a new navy blue suit with a corporate red tie. He looked up and beckoned me in.

"Hey, Jack, you sure look sharp," I said. "Maybe you're taking this engineering job too seriously."

He smiled and said he was leaving for Washington in about an hour. We both sat and he cut to the chase.

"I'm really sorry about putting you on the spot yesterday. I'd planned to catch you before the meeting, but never found the time. Sorry, but I've only got a few minutes now. If you really don't want to do this, I'll understand and get you out of it."

I shook my head. "C'mon, Jack, you know I'll do it. But I have been out of engineering for a lot of years, and there are three other Senior Fellows that would be more logical . . . and would expect to get this assignment."

"Naw. I don't really know them," he said. "And besides, I want a fresh look from an outside engineering perspective. I've been thinking about this for a while, Jon. You know, I'm absolutely amazed by the number of problems we have. On the one hand, we have excellent manufacturing capabilities. But there's no denying we have problems. Overall, I believe we have great processes and great people. I think we also have an excellent design engineering staff, plus an outstanding technology base. But somehow or other, we've lost our edge. We need to find it, Jon, and fast. I've got to believe we have the foundation to build on."

The clock was clearly ticking on my new assignment. So I started to push him. "Exactly what do you expect in one week, Jack? That's not a lot of time for any real team activity."

"Frankly, I don't really know." He seemed to think for a

second. "Do you remember Colonel Markham from Wright Pat?"

"Sure," I said. "A great customer. As I recall, he thought we walked on water." And well he should, I thought to myself. We made Markham a hero with our cost reduction, quality, and rapid response.

Jack nodded. "He's now a general in Washington and the leader of the DoD purchasing reengineering team. They're defining a standard supplier list to take effect next year. He called Ray last Friday and told him that as of today, we won't be on the list."

I felt my eyebrows lift. "What does that mean?"

"Hell, it means we will be out of business is what the hell it means. The only way we've kept our market share and not been bought is by being cheaper, faster, and better than what the big boys can do for themselves. Not being a standard supplier will change that overnight."

"Wow!" was all I could think to say, but I immediately understood the implications. The big DoD suppliers had all been consolidating over the last few years, but we'd been unaffected. Often, we'd be the IR supplier for each of the prime contractors on competing aircraft. We always won. The DoD loved to have us as part of the equation. If they had lost confidence, we were in deep trouble.

Jack leaned back in his chair. "Markham actually chewed out Ray for allowing this company to become a second rate supplier. He said we're too expensive, too arrogant, too slow, and our overhead rate has become the highest in the business. If it's any consolation, he did tell Ray our manufacturing was still the best in the industry. His comment was, 'Why in hell didn't we make engineering look like manufacturing?'"

"Bet that made Ray happy. I'm surprised he told you." Ray Collins, our CEO, had come up through engineering and was credited with our company's initiatives on Six Sigma, design automation, and process standardization.

Jack leaned forward and looked me in the eye. "Markham said we have one year to demonstrate that we can still produce to our prior levels. He also said he's been our biggest supporter and hoped we could pull it off."

"So," I said, "promoting you to lead product operations was the first step in pulling this off. In effect the customer promoted you."

"Yeah, I guess so, in a way."

Man, one helluva job lay ahead. I felt the faint sensation of butterflies in my stomach. "Jack, you still haven't given me an answer about something very important. What the hell do you expect from me in a week? You've got a year. I've got a week. Doesn't sound fair."

"The truth is, I really don't know. I'll leave it to you. Whatever you do, I need some sort of plan to shake things up and to get everyone geared for change. I set the deadline at a week to emphasize the urgency." He paused, no doubt to think. "The bare minimum would be to lay out the issues and next steps. Be bold, Jon. I'll be gone all week—meeting Markham in Washington. Then I'm on to Detroit to meet with Ford and GM. Our reputation is just as bad there. Do what you can, old friend." Jack looked at his watch. "Unfortunately, I've got to go."

After I left his office, I asked Ann if she could commandeer a conference room for me for a week. Her ready agreement wasn't much of a start, but strangely, it gave me some sense of achievement.

I decided to go by the cafeteria for some coffee on the way back to my office. Troy was there with two giant bagels.

"Troy, how many of those things you gonna eat?" I asked.

"This is a reward. I skipped the golf cart and walked yesterday."

"Well, now I see. What prompted that?"

"They had the damn carts on the path. You know I can't find

46

my ball when they do that."

I said, "Wouldn't be a problem if you'd just hit it in the fairway."

He leveled his eyes at me. "So. I see you got yourself a new job."

"How the hell did you know that?"

"My golf may stink, but I can read. There's an info sheet out about Jack taking over product operations and you leading some sort of transition team." He shook his head. "I thought you were going to coast out."

I told him I'd have to explain later. I had a meeting with Greg.

As I walked to my office, the feeling came that Troy was disappointed I didn't ask for his help. That was all I needed.

Greg was waiting. I'd been hoping that he was going to have some brilliant ideas on how to proceed, or at least he would know who could help. After I told him what Jack had said, he seemed genuinely concerned. Retirement for him was a long way off, and he had a family to support.

I stood and walked to the chalkboard. "Let's put a team together."

"Shouldn't we first have a goal?" Greg said. "What are we actually going to try to do by Monday?"

"A goal. Right," I said, realizing my utter lack of a game plan was showing.

I stood staring at the board with a marker in my hand. I'd led a lot of teams and the procedure that seemed to work best was that used by a sculptor: simply remove what doesn't look like the bear, or Venus, or whatever you were trying to create. I'd always had a pretty good sense of direction, and this approach usually worked. The problem here was that I really didn't have a vision of the end result.

Just then Donna burst into the office. Her shriek of surprise startled us.

"Whoa. What are you doing here?" she said. "And you, Greg.

Why are you grinning? For that matter, why are you here?"

I said, "Donna, I work here. Perhaps you hadn't noticed, but this is my office."

"Right, I was just opening up for the day."

I smiled. "It's a long story, Donna," I said. "This will explain." I handed her the green sheet that I'd picked up on the way back from the cafeteria. "By the way, can you take my calls while I meet with Greg?"

"Sure." She quietly closed the door when she left.

Greg said, "What's she going to do when you retire? You two have been a good team for a lot of years."

He was right to a point. Donna used to be my personal secretary, which was rather unusual for a technologist, but that was one of the perks. When we'd moved to lean, Jack stopped all that. He was now the only one in production operations who had his own secretary. In fact, he'd tried to end that, too, and was overruled. But Donna and I had been so much a part of each other's success, I supposed we'd always be linked. Her station was still outside my office and she still acted like she worked only for me. That probably wasn't right, but it worked for us. She really carried herself with great class, dressed well, but at the same time was bold and brassy. I'd tried to get her to finish her degree years ago, but a combination of kids and responsibilities prevented it. Too bad. She could have gone much farther.

"C'mon, Greg," I said. "Unlike the situation you guys have in engineering, all our secretaries are pooled. Donna hasn't worked for me in years. Not exclusively. I even make all my own travel arrangements.You know it's actually faster and easier." I looked back at the chalk board. "Okay, let's get to work. Now, what's our goal for the week? Let's see. Redesign product development, regain all our market share, and convince everyone we're right? Correct?" How stupid, but accurate this was.

Greg laughed. "No, not everyone. We only have to convince Jack."

"True," I said. "That makes it a whole lot easier."

"And," Greg said, "we don't actually have to do it. Just point things in the right direction."

Suddenly, my sculpture analogy seemed to help. Before adopting lean manufacturing, we had all kinds of improvement initiatives for warehouse automation, for inventory management systems, and for who knows what else. But none of it really helped. The lean philosophy gave us a simple model, or finished sculpture to work toward. We just stopped doing the things that didn't match the lean philosophy. Engineering had no such model against which to judge stupid ideas. If an artist has no idea what the finished sculpture is supposed to look like, how can he know what to cut and what to leave? I had no idea whether I was on the right path, but this at least gave me a place to start.

We needed to establish a foundation.

"Greg, let's start here. Can you give me a rundown of our improvement initiatives in engineering?"

Greg frowned. "Before I do that, let me ask why all the emphasis seems to be just on the engineering side? Manufacturing certainly still has its share of problems. Don't we run a risk of sub-optimization if we don't address all operations?"

I thought for a second. The last thing I needed was to reenergize the engineering versus manufacturing debate.

After some discussion, we both agreed that our fundamental problems stemmed from the fact that our products were late to the marketplace, were not meeting customer expectations, and were not diverse enough to address all the new markets for our technology. We also concluded that the problems lay not in engineering or in manufacturing, but in product development. This extended across both domains. Greg and I agreed that our production capability for recurring products was a strength. The problem was getting the right products out the first time. This was the key issue that must be established clearly in our team meeting.

"Okay, Greg. Let me rephrase my earlier question. What are all of our current initiatives in product development?"

"Well, there is the PDSP stuff."

"Fine," I said and wrote this on the left side of the board.

The PDSP, Product Development Standard Process, was an initiative started by a small group of process reengineering zealots years earlier. Doyle Mattingly, the leader, remained tremendously passionate about it. We'd spent millions over the last five years developing the details. The process was documented originally in hard copy form and had been put online last year. Its multiple layers allowed an engineer to get into as much detail as desired.

The top layer was simple process boxes. The lowest level was precise detail on how to perform every task. The complete hard copy filled three large three-ring binders. Originally designed for the military business, it had supposedly been tailored to fit the other businesses. As a result of it, Doyle managed a small army of experts, affectionately called the process police, who were assigned to all projects in order to ensure effective utilization.

I wrote "initiative" on one side of the board above PDSP and "why" on the other. "Why do we have the PDSP initiative and the standard process?" I asked.

"To put structure into how we do product development so everyone will do it the right way," he said. "I don't see where you're going here."

I said, "Does it address all of product development, including the design of production tooling? Or just the actions of the traditional engineering staff?"

"Good question," Greg responded. "It focuses strictly on the engineering team."

"Okay, so the purpose of PDSP is," I wrote under *why* on the board, *to provide design structure to the design team.*

"What's another initiative?" I asked, as I wrote "design automation" on the board.

"Right. That's one," Greg said. "The purpose is to increase the productivity and capability of the engineer."

As a company, we'd invested millions in the latest and greatest CAD capability for our engineers. Unfortunately, it seemed that the drafting department was the main user.

"Okay," I said as I wrote *engineering productivity* under the *why* column.

"I don't understand where you're going, Jon. But Six Sigma has got to be up there."

"Fine," I replied, as I wrote *Six Sigma* on the board.

As far as I was concerned, Six Sigma was an issue with respect to product development. This was an initiative that had started in manufacturing as a problem-solving methodology. It had been layered into the lean philosophy. Over the last few years, we'd developed significant data on the sigma capability of our manufacturing processes. Now we had a number of black belts throughout our facilities who systematically led teams to resolve bottleneck issues. The results in driving manufacturing variability down had been significant. As a part of this initiative, Greg had moved into engineering with a team of manufacturing experts who would work on design for manufacturability issues within the projects. To me, it was only logical this should include design for Six Sigma products. But Grant Loving had started an entire other initiative for Six Sigma design in product development that seemed to target engineering mistakes. An engineering false start was counted as a defect. All kinds of metrics were being reported that seemed to have little to do with value as measured from the customer's perspective.

I said, "So Greg, what is the purpose of the Six Sigma initiative in product development?"

There was a knock on my door, and it flew open. Donna walked in. She looked at Greg. "Why are you grinning again?"

Greg laughed. "I 'd forgotten about your bold entrances, that's all. Tell me, why do you bother knocking?"

Donna deadpanned. "I don't knock for permission. I knock to tell you to get out of the way of the door. Got a problem with that?" She turned to me, "Ann called and said she got you conference room A14 for the next two weeks. I could have done that, you know. Also, it seems that every vice president I've ever heard of has called in the last 30 minutes. Oddly enough, they all are free to work with you—just let them know when." She cleared her throat. "It would be nice if I knew what to say."

Sheesh! I hadn't thought of all the political issues. All those political animals were scrambling for position.

"Tell them." I checked myself. "Tell them that their help is too little, too late, and that Jack doesn't like them."

Donna stared at me. Then said, "And do you know that it's their secretaries that are actually calling. They expect me to be in the loop."

"Donna, how can *you* be in the loop if *I'm* not in the loop. I had no idea about any of this until yesterday afternoon." I could see by the look on her face she was more than a little irritated. I shrugged. "Okay, call them all back and set up meetings this afternoon an hour apart at their offices."

"*All* of them?" she quickly replied, "and how many hours do you think there are this afternoon?"

"Okay, just these. Nathan Jorgenson, Wayne Tillotson, Charles Osgood, Christine Dumas, and Jim Shipmann. And make it 45 minutes apart." Damn. I hated to waste time working political issues. But maybe, just maybe, they really could help. I looked at Greg. "Anybody else? Isn't that all the product line managers?"

Greg said, "I'm with Donna. That's all the time you have today."

"All right," Donna said. "I'll start them at noon, so you'll need to eat an early lunch." Then she spun on her heel and left.

Greg said, "I forgot how much fun she is. Now, where were we?"

"Six Sigma in product development. What is it and why?" I said and sat down, waiting for a long discussion. Greg spent the next 20 minutes describing various types of Six Sigma related activities in engineering. There was a software Six Sigma guru, a hardware guru, a team of engineers that attached themselves to product teams, new metrics for measuring defects for all types of engineering activities.

"Sorry, Greg, but I still don't get it." I tried to clarify my thoughts. "In my mind, Six Sigma is related to the product that we deliver to our customer. In manufacturing, it's the way we eliminate 'lean' bottlenecks in order to deliver quality. So, it's a change methodology. But it seems that in engineering, Six Sigma is about measuring. It's not about change or control in order to achieve improvement. Yesterday, before Jack took over the meeting, Jorgenson, I believe, was showing his sigma rating on initial design specifications on some new product. Why is that important to the customer? It would seem that he should only care about the final product."

I moved to the board and wrote *Quality through measurement and control* under the *why* column. "Is that close enough?" I asked.

Current Initiatives	
Initiative	**Why**
• PDSP	• To provide design structure
• Design Automation	• Design productivity
• Six Sigma	• Quality through measurement and control
(Figure 3a)	

"Sure, I guess, since I don't know where you're headed anyway."

"Fair enough." I stepped back and sat down.

Looking at the board (Figure 3a), I asked, "So, Greg, are those all our initiatives for improving engineering?"

"Probably not, but they're the biggies," he said.

"Okay, so our initiatives are about structure, efficiency,

measurement, and control." I continued. Before allowing him to respond, I asked, "And to what philosophy?"

"Go on," he prompted.

"Look. In manufacturing, we have a lean philosophy that pervades all of our thinking—systematic elimination of anything that doesn't add value for the customer. What is it in engineering? Or rather, I should say, product development?" I waited for a response. He just stared at me so I continued. "It seems that we do product development the same way we've always done it. We just try to make it more disciplined and automated. Do you remember the automated warehouse and all those damn unmanned vehicles?"

"Yeah." He laughed. "Do you remember when one almost ran over Jack?"

I grimaced. "Hell yes I remember it. Jack blamed me 'cause I was leading the software team. He pulled me out of a meeting to chew me out." The memory of it flashed in my mind. "Well, anyway, my point is that when we changed to the lean philosophy, we scrapped all that stuff. It didn't fit the lean paradigm. It seems to me that product development still hasn't found their version of lean. Am I making any sense?"

"Actually, you are." Greg still had a grin on his face. "But we all thought Jack scrapped everything because of that AGV that attacked him."

"C'mon, Greg, get serious. We're supposed to be saving a company, remember?"

"Yes, Boss. Can I have a break?"

"Good idea. I also need to see if Donna did her job."

"I'd be a little careful. She was a little upset," Greg said as we headed out.

After our break, we settled back in my office. Greg had obviously been thinking. "How about concurrent engineering? Wasn't that a fundamental change in product development thinking?"

"Theoretically, yes, it could have been," I said. "We changed from an over the transom concept to product teams, but what did we really change fundamentally about product development? We sent some of our best people, like you, into engineering to be on design teams. We did do some manufacturing planning earlier, but did we really change the perspective, or how we approached product development? Our process is that we define requirement specifications, then design specifications, then system concepts, then subsystem designs, and then manufacturing processes. We've added more structure, but have we ever designed a product, or *even tried* to design a product primarily targeted for leveraging our manufacturing technologies?"

Greg shrugged. "Basically, I'd have to say you're right. I guess what you're saying is that we need to challenge our fundamental design philosophy."

"Maybe so. Certainly, we shouldn't exclude the possibility." This conversation had made me realize there were some pretty large underlying issues.

"So, what's our goal this week for the team?" Greg said.

That was a good question. It made me realize we had to get back on track.

A thumping on the door drew our attention. Greg chuckled. "Must be Donna kicking down the door."

"If so, we're both in big trouble," I said. I opened the door, and sure enough, Donna was there with a plate with a sandwich on it in each hand.

In a monotone, she announced. "You're meeting with Jorgenson in 20 minutes. Since you're much too old to skip lunch, I brought a roast beef sandwich for you and turkey for Greg. Can't put my finger on why, but that seemed appropriate." She put down the plates and held out a hand, palm up. "That'll be $5.50 each." She withdrew her hand. "But you can pay me later."

"Thanks," I said. "Can you work with Greg this afternoon to set up for the meeting?"

"Whatever he needs," she said and closed the door.

"We're running out of time, Greg. Tonight, I'll work on the goal for the week. Right now, let's talk briefly about the team. Here's a list of functions that we need represented." I'd prepared a preliminary list the night before, and had hoped to have more time to discuss it. I slid the list over to him (Figure 3b).

Greg studied the list. "Why nobody from engineering services? Seems like the design centers, drafting, and CAD support need to be there."

"Good thinking," I said. "Let's add them. Greg, can you decide who? You know them better than I do and anyway I don't have time. I have to make political rounds."

"What criteria should I use?" he asked.

"Let's see. They should be knowledgeable, dissatisfied, creative, but not obnoxious. Remember, the goal of this team is to

---

Team Membership

Leader / Manufacturing   Jon Stevens
Manufacturing   Greg Drucker
Program Mgr (Military)
Program Mgr (Security)
Program Mgr (Automotive)
Purchasing
Hardware Engineer
Software Lead

(Figure 3b)

---

supply some sort of vision and broad plan for change, not to actually drive the change. They should be well-respected and available for the rest of the week starting tomorrow. I assume the green sheet comments on all this will clue them in that being a team member ought to be career enhancing." I'd been pleasantly surprised by how well the one page flyer, the green sheet, had done in describing our challenges and the sense of urgency. "Go ahead and call them. If you have any issues, just beep me." I looked at his empty plate. "By the way, how was your turkey sandwich?"

"Good," he said. "But I'm not sure I swallowed Donna's implications."

"Let's start the meeting at 8:30. You and I'll meet at 7:30," I said. I looked at my watch. It was time for me to leave on my political rounds.

I was convinced that my mission this week was to find engineering's version of lean, whatever it might look like. I just hoped such a thing existed.

Wednesday morning, Infrared Technologies Corporation

I pulled out of my driveway at 7 a.m. and headed to work, a little unhappy with myself. I'd planned to leave at six and beat Greg in. As often had been the case, I'd also intended to do more planning the night before, but just wasn't able to stay awake.

The meetings with the various members of the leadership team had been pretty much useless, and long. If nothing else, those guys could talk. It was disconcerting how administrative they were in their thinking. What they saw as needing attention primarily revolved around traditional organizational thinking, such as training deficiencies. While I understood their issues, resolving them would result in incremental improvements at best, nothing like what Jack was looking for. At least I'd met with them. It seemed reasonable to expect that now they'd leave me alone for the rest of the week.

I turned onto the ramp leading to the expressway and pressed on the gas.

Greg had called last night. He seemed pleased with the team. That was a relief. I'd been worried about that. I took a deep breath. Maybe things weren't so bad. It was true I had no real game plan, but there was one thing I was convinced of: product development needed a new operating philosophy. There was just no other way to make the kind of performance changes required. Finding that new philosophy would be the real goal for the week—at least finding that there was such a thing, and proving to Jack's satisfaction that the new philosophy might work for us. My job would be to keep the team focused on the big picture—whatever would lead to recreating a great company. It was Wednesday. By Friday, I'd need to have all the inputs from the team. I could then put my presentation together over the weekend for the meeting on Monday with Jack and the Leadership team. That seemed like a reasonable timeframe in which to redesign product development, I mused, as I hung a left into the parking lot.

Greg was in my office waiting when I got there. I'd hoped to have a few minutes to organize my thoughts.

"Good morning, Jon," he said. "Do we have an agenda?" No doubt Greg was concerned about our preparation.

"Kinda," I said. I motioned him toward my computer. "You type faster. Why don't you prepare it?"

He opened PowerPoint, and I began to rummage through my old slides for interesting backup material.

"Okay. I'm ready," Greg said.

"The first couple of items are easy. 'Introductions' and then 'The Goal'." I was planning on showing the metric charts that Jack presented. "Let's not define a specific goal. We can work on it as a team."

Greg jumped in. "That sounds good. Ol' Donna guessed that. She has slides of all of Jack's stuff, plus one for the team members. She's also added a few blank slides."

"Damn, she's good," I said. "After 'The Goal' on the agenda, I was thinking of adding 'Issues' and 'New Ideas'. What do you think?"

"Sounds okay." He finished typing the agenda. "Kind of sparse agenda for three days, but I can't think of anything else to add at the moment."

"Actually, I do see something missing," I said. "Add 'Product Development Scope' after 'The Goal' to get everybody focused on the product development process versus engineering. Let's go with this. We can always change it as we go. I want to keep this flexible."

Greg hit a few key strokes.

Then I said, "Okay, lets go over the team," and held his team slide (Figure 3c) so we could both look at it. "Give me a rundown on each. Why Dick Beasley? He's an old time program manager. And Troy hates him, used to gripe about him all the time."

Product Development Issues Team
- Members -

Jon Stevens	Leader / Manufacturing
Greg Drucker	Manufacturing
Dick Beasley	Program Mgr (Military)
Tim Ashcroft	Program Mgr (Security)
Vijay Suran	Program Mgr (Automotive)
Dennis Woodson	Purchasing
Carl Garcia	Hardware Systems Engineer
Lori Dunlap	Software Lead
Jay Gooding	Engineering Services

(Figure 3c)

Greg seemed ready for this question. "Because he's always been the most successful program manager from a business standpoint. He allowed the EYEHAWK program to break all the rules and they had phenomenal success. It's no secret he didn't like Troy either—thought he was a manufacturing meddler." Greg paused. His next sentence came out in a low monotone. "Doesn't like you much either, as a matter of fact."

"Oh great," I said. EYEHAWK was a 'behind-the-wall' top-secret project that had been the subject of all types of discussion in our initiative meetings. Some said that it was the most successful program ever because of the unique way they approached the project. Others said they cooked the books to justify their approach. I never got involved. It was too confusing. "So Greg, what was your take on all the EYEHAWK controversy?"

He was quick to answer. "It had the highest quality, lowest cost, and the fastest development time by far of any project I've ever seen. Of course, that couldn't really be publicized because of the secrecy. They ignored all the metrics on process usage, drawing count, specifications, and whatever. That got them in trouble, but Dick just ignored the criticism—seemed to enjoy the controversy. By the way, the engineers that actually did the project have left the company."

"Great," I said. "So the process police killed a great project?"

"That's my opinion, but Doyle obviously would have a different take, and he sits on all the management teams."

"Okay. Let's cover the rest of the team quickly. We're running out of time," I said.

"All right." Greg reeled off a rundown of the team members, obviously confident of his selections. "Tim is a young hotshot program manager that seems to have his act together. He's on everyone's list for future leadership. He thought the idea of bringing Jack in was stupid, and that having you lead this team added insult to injury. Vijay's an interesting guy—just started attending a lot of initiative meetings with a little chip on his shoulder—was in the meeting on Monday and seemed to be enjoying the moment, especially when Jack stared down Doyle."

I interrupted him. "I see. You've gotten one program manager that doesn't like me, one that thinks my selection was stupid, and one that is just plain ornery. Am I correct so far?"

Greg laughed. "Yeah, pretty much."

"Right. Let's move on."

"Dennis Woodson, you know him. He's been leading the supplier involvement initiative. He seemed a natural, and he likes you."

"Oh, good."

Greg continued. "Then there's Carl Garcia, a systems engineer that's really a great technology guy—seems to do a great job of getting the best technology into his programs without breaking the bank. Then Lori Dunlap. She's the leader of the team trying to reengineer the software part of the PD process. They're really doing some interesting things that might apply to hardware. You know Jay Gooding—he's leading the design automation stuff. I know he thinks CAD/CAM technology will solve everything, but we can't ignore it." Greg shrugged. "These people are all considered leaders by their peers. Questions?"

"No," I said. "Sounds like a good team, plus we're out of time and I need to go by the cafeteria on the way to the meeting. Also we need to stop and make a few overheads." I started gathering together the material. "Good. You have your laptop. I assume you'll be taking notes."

"Right. I knew that," he said. "I used to work for you."

"Greg, where'd you come up with our team name?" I asked. It'd be shortened to P-DIT in our acronym crazy company.

"Well, I assumed we'd at least get some semblance of success on identifying issues," Greg answered defensively. "Hell, Jon, I spent 30 minutes thinking about that last night."

"Fine," I said. The last thing I wanted to do was to debate the stupid name. "If anyone wants to spend time discussing the name, they're off the team."

Greg laughed. "Yeah. That's a good test to see if I got the right people. Remember that team that actually listed naming themselves as their major accomplishment for the month?"

We had 10 minutes before the meeting to get coffee. Sure enough, there was Troy, sitting in the back of the cafeteria, eating, and reading the paper.

Greg chuckled. "He's gotten fat. Look at his cheeks."

I decided to say hello. I hated to get to meetings early, anyway. I've never been comfortable with all the stupid small talk among people I really don't know— probably the primary driver for me being on the technical side of the business. I think of myself as a good engineer but as lacking the political charisma required for management.

Troy gave us a nod and a little wave of the hand, but I sensed his displeasure at not being involved.

"You two are off to save the company, right?"

"You bet," Greg said. "We'll let you know how the crusade turns out." A devilish smile appeared on Greg's face. "By the way, your old buddy Dick Beasley's on the team."

"You've got to be kidding." Troy said. "What an idiot." He shrugged. "It's your team. Good luck, you're gonna need it." He paused. "I have a ten o'clock tee time Saturday. You playing?"

Troy must have been testing my commitment. "We'll see," I answered honestly.

We arrived right on time at the meeting in the long, gray room with the big window overlooking the parking lot. The shades were drawn as usual. Everyone was there. The three program managers sat together talking. Lori, Carl, and Jay, the technologists, were together talking. Dennis, from purchasing, sat by himself. I smiled, thinking he'd be the first one voted off the island. I went around the room and introduced or reintroduced myself while Greg was busy setting up his laptop.

I put the agenda slide up (Figure 3d). Slowly, I began. "I know this looks like a sparse agenda for the next several days, but we're charting new territory and need to be flexible. Let's take a few minutes and introduce ourselves and our current jobs. My name is Jon Stevens and I . . . "

Product Development Issues Team
- Agenda -

- Introductions
- Goal
- Product Development Scope
- Issues
- New Ideas
- "Plan as we go"

(Figure 3d)

The introductions didn't add any insight, but they broke the ice and got everyone's voice in the game. Nobody gave a long dissertation on him or herself, which was good. It seemed like there was usually one person who really got into the intro thing.

It was interesting that the three program managers put on their best authoritative posture. Carl, Lori, and Jay sounded smart. Dennis from purchasing just seemed to appreciate being there. I smiled, thinking that if Troy had been here, he'd no doubt have been antagonistic toward the program managers.

It was my turn to speak again. "Before I talk about the goal, let me talk about team rules." I saw Greg grimace. I knew he thought I overdid this part on any team I led. "My rules are simple, but they probably run counter to those of many teams that you've been on. Everybody's comments are equal and welcome, and I encourage freethinking. But this is not a consensus-rules type of team. I've been given the responsibility and I make all final decisions. I decide when to close debates and when to move on. I believe you'll find I'm totally open to any ideas. But one thing I won't tolerate is any form of filibustering."

In my opinion, the rise of team-based management has been

positive overall, but often has resulted in the wrong kind of people getting promoted. It can also cause endless delays on decision-making and has allowed weak managers to hide behind teams. Looking around the room I saw, as usual, some folks who looked displeased by my comments, but I was surprised to see that the three program managers looked happy.

Vijay said, "Works for me. So we're more of your cabinet than a team as we've come to know and love them."

"You might look at it that way," I said without thinking through the implications. I looked around. Everyone seemed to understand. Concerned I might have been a bit too intimidating, I added, "But I expect everyone to vigorously support their position against me or anyone else. And I expect everyone to respect everyone's opinion."

Carl had a smile on his face. He said, "I am really going to miss spending a week arguing about our mission statement."

Greg's nod seemed to indicate his approval.

It was time to move on.

I said, "Before stating our goal, I need to fill you in some on Jack's meeting yesterday." I then showed them Jack's metric chart concerning IRT's dropping profitability and deteriorating market share. The nods indicated they fully appreciated the problem. This was in sharp contrast to the seeming amazement within the management team on Monday. And we wonder why Dilbert's creator has so much material to work with.

I asked for ideas on our goals for the week. What did we think we could accomplish?

I read a goal, which I regarded as a strawman, that defined the issues preventing IRT from achieving 50% improvement in costs, time to market, and overhead rate.

Then I opened up the floor for discussion.

"Why 50%?" Lori said. "In software, we think we can do better than that—at least on initial product quality. But maybe not on all three."

Carl jumped in. "Issues? Is that all we can really accomplish? Seems trivial. And what's the significance with one year?"

I decided to share with them that Jack had told me we had one year to show enough change to maintain our DoD preferred status. This had a sobering affect and the mood went from lighthearted to serious.

Dennis broke the silence. "So the promotion of Jack is a mandate for change."

"Absolutely," I said. "And we're first at bat. Jack's our only customer, and we've got 'til Monday. So what's our goal?" I suddenly had the feeling my strawman was not strong enough.

Vijay, who'd been fairly quiet until now, seemed to be interested. "Does this really surprise anyone? Over the last few years we've all watched the rise of personal bureaucracies, the lack of anyone taking personal responsibility. And everybody seems perfectly okay with it. I don't know Jack except by reputation, but I can tell you I do like how he handled the Monday meeting. If we're serious, I think our goal should be something like this, 'To define a product development environment that will consistently produce products that meet all of our customers' requirements in half the time that it takes today'."

Dick added, "I like that, but it only focuses on the customer. Our shareholders care about a profit—that needs an equal focus."

"Why are you only focusing on improvement in cycle time?" Lori said. "How about cost and quality? Our Six Sigma initiative is a huge investment."

Vijay defended his position. "Because the customer couldn't care less about our initiatives for Six Sigma, cost reduction, or cycle time improvement. They just want the product with the right features, right quality, the right price, at the right time. I added a cycle time reduction because unless we have a consistent and fast time to market, we'll never have an effective process for managing our resources and developing a consistent flow of products." His exasperation showed. "We never make a schedule around here. I think I'm a good program manager, but for the life of me, I can't make it happen on time. Something is fundamentally wrong."

I'm not sure why, perhaps it was Vijay's passion, but dead silence followed his speech.

As what he said sunk in, I had to admit it made sense. So I walked to the flip chart and proposed a new goal.

To define a product development environment that consistently produces a product in half the time it takes today, while achieving ROI goals and meeting all our customers' requirements.

In an effort to shut off further debate, I acknowledged the change. "What I like about this is that it effectively addresses the three customers of the product development process: our actual customers, our shareholders, and the manufacturing process. What Vijay said about consistent cycle time schedules is critical for the manufacturing process. We can never plan our production schedules because the product is always released late with unresolved technical issues. Now, unless someone sees something I've missed, I want to move on. I don't plan to get hung up on this goal statement. If we veer off slightly, we can always modify it."

Dennis had a puzzled look on his face. "I don't understand your comment about the manufacturing process being a customer of the product development process."

I said, "Thank you for the lead in, Dennis. Let me see if the next discussion will answer your question, all right?"

He nodded.

I said, "I added Product Development *scope* to the agenda as a level setting on what product development entails. Over the last few years, we've tried to change from a functional perspective to a process perspective—where the process is the primary vehicle for improvement. I think it's important we make sure we all understand the scope of our effort from a process perspective. I hope everyone realizes that when Jack took over the engineering reins, he took on two roles: one is the functional role over all of the engineering functions, the other is the position of owner of the product development process. We're addressing only the process. This is the one he cares about, so we need to make sure we're always talking product development process and not the engineering departments." I looked from one team member to another. "Does everyone remember a few years ago when we were on a kick to reengineer all of our processes?"

A few groaned, and others nodded.

I continued, "I know we didn't achieve a lot of gains from the reengineering projects, but I really liked the process focus. It emphasized that the efficient flow of work from and to the customer is what's important—not the efficiency of individual functions within the process. Optimizing individual functions doesn't optimize the overall process. I thought the high level mapping activity that defined our major processes and the interfaces was very good for defining scope."

I put up the high-level process map that had been developed and approved at the corporate level (Figure 3e).

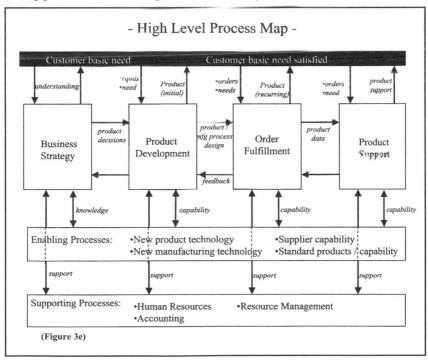

(Figure 3e)

"This map describes the logical interfaces between our major processes. Unless someone has a problem, I propose we use this to define our 'Product Development' scope."

I saw confused looks on some.

Greg said, "Jon, this chart is logically correct, and it's fine to use it to define our scope. It correctly identifies the work, not organizations, as the avenue for improvement. But . . . " He stopped to frame his words. "Management never really accepted this chart from that perspective. They all just assumed it was a renamed organizational chart. 'Product Development' was another name for 'Engineering'. 'Order Fulfillment' was another name for 'Production Operations'. Nothing really changed. Look at my organization, Producibility, for example. In order to get a concurrent engineering perspective, you, being a manufacturing organization, moved my entire group of 25 manufacturing engineers into the engineering organization where we were largely ignored both personally and professionally. If we were really process focused, we should have remained in the manufacturing organization and worked in the product development process. Also, how about actual tool design? It's still in the manufacturing box, but should be a part of product development. But there's no way Jack was going to let Grant Loving have the tool designers. So, if we use that chart as our scope, and I agree we should, I think we need to recognize we're crossing organizational boundaries."

"So be it." I said. Now was not the time to worry about the organizational implications.

Dick was next to speak. "I always doubted the value of this high-level mapping stuff, but I'll admit it does make a difference on how you perceive the work within the process boxes. Only when you separate the responsibilities of managing the people from managing the work do you really achieve a process focus."

Nodding, I put up the next layer of the map that defined the major steps inside the product development process. (Figure 3f).

"This chart completes the scope definition by defining the primary steps in product development. This becomes our baseline for improvement." I looked from one individual to the next. " Anyone see anything I'm missing?"

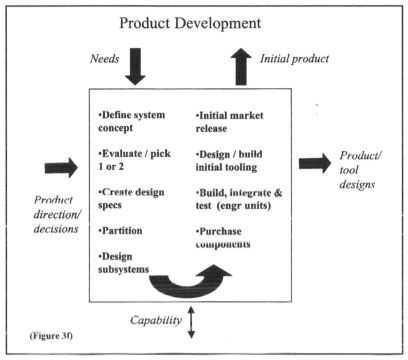

(Figure 3f)

"That's okay," Carl said. "As long as you recognize that only our best projects follow that process efficiently. Most are still functionally oriented."

I said, "Okay, let me ask another question. Can our most efficient programs, by following those steps, meet the goals we just laid out. Can they reverse the trend Jack's charts showed?"

After a few minutes of discussion, it was apparent, and frustrating, to realize that our best projects, with our best processes, would at best do nothing more than make us average.

"Okay," I said. "Then let's assume this chart represents our baseline for change. It's process focused. It defines our major steps, and it defines interfaces to other major company processes. Let me ask another question."

Tim laughed. "Jon, we were actually hoping for some answers, as opposed to more questions."

I said, "Humor me for a few more minutes. Remember, I haven't been in design for fifteen years. Would somebody define the development system for me? I see the steps, but what's the system?"

I saw brows furrow.

"Maybe I should rephrase that. I'm sure I could make a chart as simple as this one (Figure 3f) to show the steps for passing a law in Congress, and I'd swear it should be done in weeks. But the 'system' somehow takes months or years. When I was in design years ago, I believe I followed the same steps back then, but we did it a lot faster than today. So what's our development system?" I looked around. "Carl, you're a systems engineer. Describe our system. Whatever it is should be our real baseline."

"I see your point," Carl said. "Our system is actually the entire supporting infrastructure we've built around product development. We have the PDSP standard process that ensures the engineer follows all the correct procedures—in fact he has to produce a plan and report on his compliance. Likewise, he has to have a manufacturability plan to support concurrent engineering requirements. He has quality requirements and metrics and CAD/CAM standards to meet. He also has a standard task based timeline he must report on at each design review. And of course, we have our automated design specification control system that the engineers have to keep up to date with their design data."

"So, in effect," I said, "our product development system is the process along with all the structure we put around it. That entire pile of stuff becomes the system." No sense debating this further. All I wanted at this point was affirmation that our team was all on the same page. "Okay, we have our goal and understand our scope within the overall high level process map." Turning to Dennis, I said, "Does this answer your concern that manufacturing, or the order fulfillment process to be more accurate, is actually a customer of product development? We get and deserve a prompt and accurate recipe for building the product."

"Absolutely," he said. "This makes sense, particularly when you think of it in terms of process and not functions."

I asked, "Any other questions, comments, or concerns before we move on?"

"Just one clarification," Tim said. "Concerning our scope, I'm assuming from these charts that product development officially begins when a customer's needs are known, and that the decision to go is made from the business strategy process. And I assume the process ends when the initial product is delivered to the customer off of a real production line—even if it's at a rather low production rate. Is this correct?"

"That seems logical," I said. "Those points are clearly measurable for our goal and are totally within the confines of the PD process as we've defined it. It'd seem more pure if it started as soon as sufficient customer needs were known to start, but that's somewhat dependent on the 'business strategy' sub process, so for now, let's make that assumption."

I saw them nod, but even so was somewhat concerned we were too narrow. Hell, we needed to move on. I looked at my watch. "Okay," I said. "Let's break for lunch. We'll start back here in forty-five minutes, okay? Next, we'll talk about issues."

When I arrived at the cafeteria, I was pleased to see that almost everyone had found one large table and seemed to be getting along fine. They seemed to be okay with our direction, too. Nothing is worse than leading a team that's out of touch with each other or me.

So far, so good.

Back in the room, before we started on our own list of issues, everyone seemed anxious to hear the issues I'd gotten from the managers the day before. That had not been my plan, but I was overruled. The truth is, I think everyone wanted a break from having to do any real thinking. The night before, I'd summarized the lists from my meetings, but had left the names off.

I shrugged. "Okay, here's their list." (Figure 3g) My question to each of them was what, in their opinion, was the primary issue that needed to be resolved in order to meet the challenges that Jack had laid out."

ISSUES
(from leadership team individually)

- Slow drafting response time / CAD capability
- Systems problems: CAD database issues
- Staffing delays from other projects
- Always changing requirements; marketing problems
- Deteriorating engineering capability
- Too many manufacturing problems
- Technology is not ready

(Figure 3g)

After a couple of minutes of looking at the leadership team's issues, Vijay broke the silence. "You know, the fact that these are their issues may be the primary issue."

The chuckles from around the room put my mind at ease. I'd been afraid this set of what I considered trivial problems might be considered significant by the group.

I took down the slide and said, "Okay, let's brainstorm. I want to identify the systemic issues causing our poor business metrics. I'm not going to follow normal brainstorming rules. I want each of you to raise the issue and elaborate on what you mean. But to make the list, it must be seconded. I'm hoping that when we've finished, every item on our list will be resolved by whatever our new PD environment is. And that we can explain why in a way Jack will believe. Who wants to start?"

Vijay jumped in. "I was serious a minute ago about our so-called leaders not having any ideas as to the real issues. That's a major issue. They're clueless."

I smiled. "Vijay, do you really want me to stand up in front of those guys Monday and say they're clueless?"

Dick said, "Hell, why not? You're retiring. I second it."

"How's?" I said, and wrote on the flip pad under systemic issues, *"Project management has become too administrative."*

"Okay, if that's the best you can do," Vijay said. I think he was enjoying my discomfort. "But the statement implies that I'm also too administrative, and I don't think I'm clueless."

Greg laughed. "But you're probably on your way. You just have to be promoted one or two more times before you become totally clueless."

"Unfortunately," Dick said, "you're probably right. I'm almost totally administrative at this point, and I was—still am—a good engineer. In a few years, though, I'll have totally lost my technical competence. Anyway, your issue statement is okay."

Carl had a puzzled look on his face. "I've always wondered why upper management so often seems out of touch with the technical aspects of the business. I think what we're saying here is that every promotion has driven them further from the technical or product side. Therefore, it's somewhat preordained that they'll eventually become technically clueless."

"I think you're right," Dick said. "The issue is not that upper level management is incompetent. Our product development philosophy is based more upon administration excellence than technical excellence, and it's getting worse."

This exchange gave me confidence in the wording of this issue.

Tim raised his hand. "Here's another issue. Our productivity in terms of value-added efforts absolutely sucks. I don't know what the number is percentage wise, but it is very low."

Jay, who'd been very quiet but attentive, piped up. "I think I know what it is. We ran a two-month study last year on twenty engineers as a part of our CAD requirements team, using that little time measuring device where they keep track of their time while on real design projects. The results showed twenty percent value-added against what the customer would consider value-added. That means those engineers spend 80% of their time doing work they don't believe is relevant to developing the product. The reason you don't know is that Grant squelched the results."

"Twenty percent? No way," I said. "That's horrendous."

"Heck, I'm surprised it's that high," Greg put in.

I turned to the board and added, ***"Value-added engineering effort is approximately 20%."***

"This is ridiculous," I said. "This in itself is a big enough issue to justify a wholesale change. Are our competitors all this bad?"

"Pretty much," Jay said. "Somehow, it's pretty consistent across product development—at least of the companies we're familiar with."

Vijay said, "With one big exception. I believe Toyota is more like 80% value-added both for engineers and managers."

I looked at him. From his expression, there was a lot more behind that statement that he hadn't said. If it was true, it said we really were lousy. But it also said there was hope.

"Vijay, can you expand on this?" I said.

"Oh, sure," he said. "But I think we need to finish getting the issues on the table."

Carl, who'd been waiting patiently for his turn, raised the next one. "Our project reviews are a joke. Everybody lies about the real status of their programs, and everyone accepts the lies. It takes time away from critical activities, and we're always preparing information that's basically meaningless."

I saw agreement around the room. This exercise had definitely generated some passion. They agreed that the classic example was drawings. One of the primary indicators of whether the project schedule was being met was the percentage of drawings completed. Everyone prepared the simple drawings first to give the illusion of real progress. It was a shell game everyone played.

Dick, while seconding this, underscored the idiocy of it. "Do you remember the problem I got into when we chose not to do drawings on the EYEHAWK until the end of the project? We were actually ahead of schedule on completing our castings and releasing the difficult databases to manufacturing, but we were behind on releasing our simple drawings. I don't think anybody really ever understood where we were."

As I wrote, **"Ineffective design reviews,"** on the flip chart, I wondered how we'd stayed in business as long as we had.

"Okay, this is good. What's next?" I said.

Greg took up the gauntlet. "Here's my pet issue. We say we do concurrent engineering, but we really don't. We have advisors, like our producibility engineers, our Six Sigma blackbelts, and other roving bands of experts. Their primary job is to critique and advise the design engineers as early as possible in the design process. We always start our designs from the same perspective, a systems engineering technical perspective, and then try to make whatever it is as producible as possible along the way. Real concurrent engineering would allow the different perspectives, including manufacturing, all to be considered equally from the start. That's why we always arrive at the most technical and expensive solutions. We have very technical systems engineers. Sorry Carl, but you guys are too smart for our own good. Of course, that's just my humble opinion."

Carl said, "I never really thought of it from that perspective, but I think you're right. I'll second it."

Dennis added, "Can we consider our supplier base a part of this problem? We have great suppliers with excellent technical knowledge of our components, but we only use their expertise to tell us we screwed up and how we should have done it."

I added, *"Designs always from one perspec-tive, not real concurrent engineering (including suppliers),"* to the flip chart.

Dick spoke up again. "These issues may go on forever. Here's another. We have very little learning between projects. We continually reinvent the wheel, or worse, repeat our mistakes. We have our MIS systems, our engineering databases, but we have no real transfer of knowledge across projects, or any real reuse of our good components. Also, our manufacturing knowledge and requirements aren't really communicated well enough for any real design leverage to occur. It's ridiculous, but I guess it's just not in our culture."

I looked around the room. Heads nodded, so I added, *"Minimal learning between projects."*

Tim added, "On a related note, most of our engineers only complete one engineering cycle. Therefore, they don't have much of a learning curve. Our projects take too long. We have too many side assignments, and our engineers all want to become supervisors quickly. And as we've already discussed, in the upper ranks you become primarily an administrator. Our technical ladder is pretty good, but it's not extensive enough. Thank goodness our competitors operate the same way." He shook his head. "I'm sure glad the medical profession is different."

So I added, *"Design engineers have very little design experience,"* to our list.

"How about schedules?" Dennis said. "We spend a lot of time making our PERT charts. Then halfway through the project they're out of date, totally unrealistic, and always somehow indicate that purchasing has screwed up."

This issue caused the group to plunge into a lively discussion about the deficiencies of our scheduling system. The upshot was we were spending a small fortune on creating a link between our standard PDSP process and Microsoft Project. The goal was automatic time-based management charts based on generic tasks that the process police felt everyone should follow.

I called for an end to the discussion and added *"Inaccurate, unmaintainable scheduling system,"* to our list.

The group was silent for a moment. Then Lori spoke up. "I'm not sure if this is an issue or if it comes about as a result of the others, but we continually have these long loopbacks from the end of the design process to the front. These result in changes in some of our original assumptions, and this impacts on other things, causing communication issues, and so on. It seems like it always happens, which to my mind makes it a systemic problem."

A good deal of discussion ensued, the bottom line of which was that it was at the same base level as the other issues. Vijay in particular insisted it was not just a result of the issues already identified, but a causal issue on its own. So I added, *"Systemic long design decision loopbacks,"* thinking that somehow I was playing into Vijay's hand.

Looking at our list, I believed we'd identified enough issues with our product development process to ensure our incompetence. The fact that our competitors seemed to have many of the same issues was comforting in a way, but also disturbing. Maybe product development was inherently an inefficient process. Exploring this possibility had to be our next task.

I looked at my watch. We'd gone a while without a break. This was a good place to stop so I asked everyone to judge whether they were comfortable that the critical issues were on the table. They agreed that if we could resolve these we should be able to generate a process capable of meeting our goals.

After the break and a few minutes of discussion, I told them it was time to move on. Some other issues were discussed: poor metrics, our specification process and tools, our CAD capability, but we decided these were all corollaries of larger issues or not that critical.

Lori seemed a little frustrated about the negativity of what we'd been discussing and asked what the good things were that we could build on. That seemed like a reasonable approach, and it didn't take us long to recognize that we had excellent engineers overall and the ability to attract them. We had a strong Six Sigma methodology for continuous improvement, excellent black belt and quality training programs, and an excellent design automation strategy. We also believed that we had excellent technical leaders who had not yet lost their technical excellence. This turned out to be a good exercise. We all realized we had the basics to rebuild a great product development process.

I put the agenda slide back up. The next item, "New Ideas," was the part I was worried most about. Everything so far was a prelude to this. Now we had to get down to determining how we were going to move forward. The day so far had been productive. We'd done an excellent job of identifying why we were so bad.

What to do about it—that was the question.

"As you can see," I said, "it's now time to figure out how to fix these issues. I hope you have some ideas. Jack did mention that he thought we should make engineering look more like manufacturing. I want to explore that. Maybe there is some leverage." I was a little concerned about pushing this hard because everyone knew I was from manufacturing, and could push back just on general principle. But I did believe there was some potential in this approach. At the bare minimum, it should open up the discussion.

Dennis raised his hand. "What about all our current improvement initiatives? We're spending a lot of money on them. Isn't it arrogant of us to jump right past them? Do we know for a fact that they're not trying to resolve the same issues?"

He had a point. I indeed had moved right past that possibility.

"Okay," I said. "That's a reasonable question. How do we want to do that?"

"Why not make a matrix?" Lori suggested. "And we can test our initiatives logically against the issues. I'm curious how that

78

will turn out."

"All right," I said. That seemed logical. I went to the board and listed our issues on the left and our current initiatives along the top, then created a legend across the bottom. "What we can do is use these codes to identify the impact of the initiative on that issue. It can resolve it, it can improve it, it can have no impact or it can be negative. Is this reasonable?"

They agreed.

I asked, "How about Six Sigma? What's the impact?"

After what seemed a long pause, Greg, our only black belt, said that he'd take a crack. "This is really interesting, but in my opinion, our Six Sigma strategy does not resolve any of our issues. It probably helps some, but more in a way that masks them." He went to the board and made his ranking.

Everybody agreed his ranking was reasonable, but more important, everyone agreed that Six Sigma was a great problem solving and improvement methodology. It simply didn't provide the basis for resolving any of our fundamental issues in product development (Figure 3h).

Current Initiative Effectiveness

	6-Sigma	Process Standardization	Design Automation
Administrative leadership	I		
Low value-added effort	0		
Ineffective design reviews	0		
Pseudo concurrent engineering	I		
Minimal learning between projects	0		
Low engineering experience	I		
Inaccurate scheduling	0		
Long design loop backs	0		

R = resolves   I = Improves   0 = no change   -- = makes worse

(Figure 3h)

I said, "Okay, any volunteers who want to tackle what our

PDSP initiative has done to help resolve our issues?"

"Not a damn thing," Dick said. The other two program managers nodded in agreement. "Actually, it's made some of our issues worse. Here's my ranking."

Dick went to the board and marked his ranking. After a few minutes of discussion, agreement was reached on the impact. Again, everyone was in accord that our standard process had not resolved any of our fundamental issues (Figure 3i).

"Jay, you're our automation guy. What's your ranking for design automation?"

"Okay," he said. "Here's what I think. I don't think design automation actually resolves any of our primary issues, but I think it does help transfer knowledge across projects—even though most people don't take advantage of our legacy databases. But it has to help."

Current Initiative Effectiveness			
	6-Sigma	Process Standardization	Design Automation
Administrative leadership	I	--	
Low value-added effort	0	0	
Ineffective design reviews	0	--	
Pseudo concurrent engineering	I	--	
Minimal learning between projects	0	0	
Low engineering experience	I	0	
Inaccurate scheduling	0	I	
Long design loop backs	0	0	

R = resolves   I = Improves   0 = no change   -- = makes worse

(Figure 3i)

Everyone agreed in principle.

I'm sure I wasn't the only one who was amazed that none of our primary initiatives were judged effective at all in addressing our underlying problems. Our initiatives would improve the issues in some cases, but we all felt that the improvement was generally superficial—more of a band-aid than a real cure (Figure 3j).

I felt we'd gone as far as needed in reviewing our current initiatives. It was time to start exploring new ideas. Deep down, I was glad our initiatives didn't appear to be the answer. I knew Jack wanted a fresh start, but I didn't feel I could force the issue.

I said, "Earlier, I mentioned that Jack indicated he wanted Product Development to look more like manufacturing. We don't have to go that route, but we'd better be ready to answer the question. Any ideas?"

"I've got one," Carl responded. "In fact, I think we've answered the question with the issues we've just identified. If they aren't the same in development and in production, or if they have to be resolved in different ways, then trying to make the processes the same obviously will fail."

Current Initiative Effectiveness			
	6-Sigma	Process Standardization	Design Automation
Administrative leadership	I	--	0
Low value-added effort	0	0	0
Ineffective design reviews	0	--	0
Pseudo concurrent engineering	I	--	0
Minimal learning between projects	0	0	I
Low engineering experience	I	0	0
Inaccurate scheduling	0	I	0
Long design loop backs	0	0	0

R = resolves   I = Improves   0 = no change   -- = makes worse

(Figure 3j)

Tim concurred and suggested we try matching them up.

"Okay, how about administrative leadership?" I asked, unsure whether this exercise made sense and would convince Jack.

"Totally different," Carl said. "Think about it. In manufacturing—excuse me, 'order fulfillment'—administrative leadership could be okay because the main emphasis is executing defined tasks to an established recipe. In development, the main emphasis is defining new solutions, testing, and reacting to results. Seems to me this takes a totally different leadership approach."

Carl's comments reinforced what was on the high-level map.

"Makes sense, Carl. Keep going," I urged.

Dick jumped in. "Carl, I agree and the same holds true for the value-added issue. In manufacturing, the value is in the parts that are being made. In development, the value is in the knowledge. These are totally different. It's silly to think the same process would optimize both."

Carl good-naturedly chastised Dick for using the term 'manufacturing' instead of the process term 'order fulfillment.' Then he moved on to the next issue. "Design reviews are not appropriate for 'order fulfillment', so there's no comparison there. Effective concurrent engineering is not an issue. Likewise, learning between projects is important for both, but what you learn is totally different. Manufacturing is about techniques for better quality and lower costs. Engineering is about products or components in addition to better design capability." He shrugged. "Sorry about using the functional terms, but it is easier."

I agreed with Carl and added that our Six Sigma strategy had been a major driver for our continuous learning in production , but did not appear to be a natural driver in development.

Carl nodded and continued. "Our level of engineering experience is not a factor in production, since the focus is on repetition and automation, not knowledge or expertise. And the last issue, long engineering loopbacks, is also not a factor in order fulfillment. The bottom line is that there's no way product development and production—or I should say, order fulfillment— ought to look at all the same. Maybe that's the problem. We've tried to do that too much. Hell, Jon, I believe I can even convince Jack of it."

Lori said, "You've convinced me, Carl. They're too different. Heck, even if I wasn't convinced, I'd be too tired to argue. Can we go home now, Jon?"

I looked at my watch. It was after five. I told everyone to think hard about new ideas for tomorrow morning.

Vijay asked if he could have five minutes before we broke, and then plunged right in. "I have a request for tomorrow. We've done a good job today in identifying and understanding issues. No doubt can exist that we're a screwed up company. I suspect that we'll be throwing out a lot of ideas tomorrow about how to proceed, which is good. But I have a woman who works for me, Jan Morris, who's been looking at new paradigms for product development for a couple of years. I'm certain she could add some real value to our discussion."

"Wait a minute," I said. "Why was she doing this? Under whose direction? How come no one knows about it?"

"She was our representative on a National Center for Manufacturing Sciences project," Vijay said. "I asked her to do it since she seemed as though she wanted to get involved in an outside company effort." He shrugged. "I wanted to keep her motivated. She's an excellent engineer."

I was familiar with NCMS. It was fairly active in manufacturing, too. Being a consortium that provides companies with an avenue to develop research to benefit all the participants, most of the findings, even those that might do some real good, are never implemented by its members.

"Anyway," Vijay continued, "she thought the project had some very good results, and I got her on the agenda for the Process Steering Team. She got absolutely nowhere—nobody gave her any encouragement whatsoever. She felt the team was rude. It was obvious they had no interest in anything she had to say. I can verify this because I was there. She's now actively looking outside the company." He shook his head. "Really ticked me off, I can tell you. It's one of the reasons I decided to get involved in all this."

I turned to Greg. "What the hell is the Process Steering Team?"

Greg frowned. "Because we have so many initiatives, Grant formed this team to ensure coordination between all the factions. The team also does the first round of ranking for funding initiatives. Doyle chairs it. I'm not surprised about Vijay's comments. I'm sure they saw her report as a threat to their initiatives—it never had a chance. I'm sure she had no idea about the minefield she walked into."

"Hard to believe," I said. Then, turning to Vijay, "I'd love to hear her ideas. Can you get her to come in tomorrow morning?"

"Somehow, I doubt it. She it clear she wants no part of any of this—just wants out." He paused. "Maybe if you called her."

"Okay, what's her number?" I went to the phone in the back of the room.

"Hello, this is Jan."

"Jan, this is Jon Stevens. I'm here with Vijay Suran. We're on a team to define a new approach for product development. He says you might be able to give us some insight based on the NCMS project you were on. I'd like to invite you to come to our meeting tomorrow and brief us."

A long pause took me by surprise.

"Jon," she said. "I appreciate your asking. I saw the green sheet on your team and the reorg. I'm glad Vijay's on your team, but I also know that the only reason you're calling is because Vijay suggested it. I'd really prefer not to get involved."

"Whoa. What can I do to change your mind? It'll only take a couple hours of your time."

She laughed. "Tell you what. I'll think about it, but I doubt I'll change my mind. Now, if Jack Holder called and asked me nicely, well, maybe that would do it."

"I see," I said and hung up. I felt the urge to pick my chin up off the floor.

"What did she say?" Vijay asked "Didn't sound like you won her heart."

"No," I said. "She must be one frustrated lady. Said she'd come if Jack called and asked her. Do you have her home number?"

"Actually, I do," he said and took out his organizer. "Who're you calling?"

"Jack" I said, as I dialed a cell phone. "He said to call if I needed anything."

DISCUSSION

A case for change and an aggressive target have been established. The issues that prevent the current operational environment from meeting objectives have been discussed and documented. Without first taking these steps, no good basis would exist for evaluating the proposed environment, nor would there be a logical rationale for discarding the old one. It is important to follow this course from the perspective of change management because the workers targeted for change are certainly going to ask questions, inwardly and perhaps outwardly.

In this case study, IRT Corporation again did several things right. Since successful change is so difficult to achieve, it is important to adhere to the principles listed below, though how this is achieved is immaterial.

1. Provide clear communication of pending change.

At IRT, this was accomplished by a major reorganization, and the subsequent assignment and communication that Jon was to lead a change team. The entire organization was put on notice of pending changes and a sense of urgency was established. The changes weren't announced, just the need for changes.

2. Set quantifiable stretch goals.

If major change is required, business targets that can be measured and are well beyond current capability must be established, communicated, and accepted. This is publication of the case for action. Workers do not want change for the sake of change. They do not want change based on what they perceive as management's whim. But they will accept change to meet a real need of the company.

3. Understand the scope of change.

The story went into detail concerning the high-level mapping in order to define the scope of product development. How the necessary mapping is done is not important, but clearly understanding the scope of change is. Traditionally, improvements target functional areas that can actually suboptimize the overall process as seen from the customer's perspective, such as engineering. Product development is an overall process that includes all functional areas required to produce and deliver the product. This scope and understanding must be well communicated.

4. Assign an open-minded leader.

Arrogant leadership ranks high on the list of reasons that change often fails. If the scope of change had been in the manufacturing arena, for example, Jon might have been much less open-minded than in the world of product development. He likely would have assumed the answers without even asking the questions. He may not have challenged conventional thinking. These are hazardous pitfalls in the world of change management. Also, a leader assigned to change the product development methodology must be able to assimilate and coalesce technical information. It is highly likely that this would be beyond the capabilities of most administrators.

5. Select a team (microcosm) with extensive and recognized knowledge across the environment.

It goes without saying that before change can occur the acceptance and compliance of individuals will be required. This can be facilitated by engaging the efforts of a support team with broad technical knowledge across the scope of product development. The team should represent a microcosm of the entire organization targeted for change. It must possess the knowledge of that organization and be able to draw upon more knowledge as needed. The team's activities should be visible to all who will be affected, and individual members should be well respected. When this is the case, the team and its members can be highly effective in directing and leading the change.

The ability of the current processes, organizations, and improvement initiatives to achieve the defined targets must be realistically assessed. All too often, wishful thinking and the lowest path of resistance overshadow honest evaluation. In particular, look for issues that are systemic to the operational philosophy. For example, in manufacturing, excessive or out-of-date inventory would never be fully resolved simply by improvements in inventory management, but only by inventory reduction within a lean operational philosophy. The issues defined in this case study are typical of systemic product development issues; they will not be resolved simply by process improvements.

6. Define and understand the core issues.

The ability of the current processes, organizations, and improvement initiatives to achieve the defined targets must be realistically assessed. All too often, wishful thinking and the lowest path of resistance overshadow honest evaluation. In particular, look for issues that are systemic to the operational philosophy. For example, in manufacturing, excessive or out-of-date inventory would never be fully resolved simply by improvements in inventory management, but only by inventory reduction within a lean operationing philosophy. The issues defined in this case study are typical of systemic product development issues; they will not be resolved simply by process improvements.

In summary, with these steps taken, the organization will be able to extract, analyze, and document the capabilities of the current processes and the initiatives that will be needed to meet the targets. The basis for measurement will be established first and the gaps identified. Then the framework for change management can be provided. With these steps accomplished, new operational paradigms can be evaluated honestly and objectively.

Chapter 4

Seeing the Opportunity
(The Power of Vision)

A high level vision of the future environment that will achieve the business targets provides focus for the change effort. If the targets require dramatic changes, the vision must provide a clear discontinuity from current practices. Without such a framework, functional biases will likely suboptimize the potential benefits. In product development, a new vision will typically manifest itself as a new operational paradigm or philosophy.

Thursday morning, Infrared Technologies Corporation

The drive to work had been anything but simple. I'd thought an accident was the problem, but it was just some stupid stalled car attracting rubberneckers. Sometimes human nature is really strange. I have to admit I also gawked as we drove slowly by.

I'd hoped to get in early so I could call Jan before the meeting. Last night, having Jack call her had seemed a good idea, but now I was having second thoughts. Oh well, what's done is done I decided. If she didn't show up I hoped Vijay could cover the NCMS stuff.

Overall, I felt fairly good about our progress. I really liked the team—smart, active. Nobody was obnoxious. I wasn't confident we were going to live up to Jack's expectations, but I felt certain we'd be able to verify his opinion that our current initiatives and process weren't going to solve our fundamental problems.

I stopped by my office only long enough to brief the ever-curious Donna about our progress and to retrieve my notes from the day before. I went by the cafeteria. I don't function well without a twelve ounce Styrofoam cup of coffee.

Troy was there as usual. He waved me over. It was obvious to me he couldn't stand not being involved.

A little smirk on his face, he said, "So. How're you getting along with Dick Beasley?"

"Just fine," I answered honestly. "He's really contributing. Gotta go, Troy. Got held up by an accident."

I could feel his frown as I headed off. No doubt he wanted to debate Dick's contributions.

I arrived right at eight o'clock. Everyone was already there, including a new lady sitting next to Vijay—Jan, I assumed. She looked younger than I'd envisioned—quite attractive and professional. She stared at me as though she wanted to chew me out but couldn't due to protocol.

The room fell silent when I entered.

"So, Mr. Stevens," she said, "would you like to hear about my evening last night?"

"I've a feeling I'm going to whether I want to or not."

In a very calm and matter of fact tone she said, "Well, let's see. The phone rang and my husband, who really doesn't like men calling me at night, answered and gave one Mr. Jack Holder a third degree interrogation. It might still be going on if I hadn't walked into the room. I can't believe you did that." She shrugged. "I still don't remember what exactly he said or how I responded. He's very persuasive, however. So here I am."

"If it's any consolation, I worried about it all last night. It seemed like a good thing to do at the time. You did tell me you'd come if he were to call."

"Actually," she said, "my husband said that wasn't such a bad thing to have the executive vice president know who you are. He's probably right—depending on what I said and how I said it.

Actually, Jack seemed very nice—a lot different from what I expected."

I smiled as I put the agenda slide back up to reset everyone's attention. "Yesterday, we set the goal for our effort, reworked our high-level map to set the scope of product development, defined the critical development issues, and tested our current initiatives against those issues. We concluded that our current process, even given the best that all of our initiatives could accomplish, would never be able to resolve any of the issues." I looked around the room. "Anyone had second thoughts?" I waited for a response, then said, "I can tell you all, this was a big revelation for me."

Dick said, "And for me. So much so that we must be missing something. How could we be spending so much money, year after year, on improvement initiatives that have no real chance of resolving the fundamental issues?"

Jan said, "I think I'll be able to answer that as I walk through all my stuff." She was obviously ready to take the floor.

I said, "Our next and last agenda item is new ideas and what to do with them. Let's let Jan walk us through the NCMS project. At minimum this should give us a strawman that, hopefully, we can build on or use as a launching point." I looked at her. "It's all yours. Take all the time you need. Within reason of course."

As Jan was walking to the front of the room, she said, "If I am taking too long, I assume you will have Jack call me to hurry up." I was starting to like her and wondered whether she was related somehow to Donna.

She opened her folder, and I spotted a two-inch stack of overheads.

"Don't worry," she assured us, "I'm not going to punish you by showing all of these. I brought them all so I could mix and match them as I need to. Do you realize that this is two years of work paid for by the company that nobody, until now, has cared about? I might be young but I know stupid when I see stupid."

She cleared her throat. "Actually, I'm going to try to use very few of these slides. I know you're interested in just a brief overview this morning. But as you can see, I have a lot of detail." She held up a thick, bound report. "This is a copy of the final document. It goes into a lot of detail on the overall project results. I have several copies that nobody has ever asked to see. I'm also sure I can retrieve many more that are gathering dust on shelves of people that received personal copies."

She continued with some background on the project. "The goal was to investigate world class companies to find fundamentally different product development processes. The search was for ways to dramatically improve cycle time, quality, and cost. The companies involved included defense companies, automobile suppliers, and some general manufacturing companies. Toyota was the impetus for the project. That company is generally considered to have a great product development process as measured against its competitors. A man named Dr. Allen Ward had studied the Toyota system while on the faculty of the University of Michigan. He's given a number of workshops on Toyota's system and was a consultant to the NCMS project. Our goal, however, was also to find other companies, not just Toyota, with exemplary product development capabilities. We weren't looking for new tools or techniques, but rather entirely different operational philosophies.

"And did you find any others?" Jay asked.

"No," she said. "We found several companies with interesting leadership or process approaches, but who were still basically in the traditional operational paradigm. They're documented in our report, but I don't think you are looking for tactical solutions. Correct?"

I nodded in agreement.

Jan put up her first slide. She looked at Dick. "You asked how we could possibly be spending all our improvement dollars on activities that have no chance of truly making a difference. I believe the answer is simple and is based on our approach toward product development. In our case, and in the case of every company we looked at except Toyota, product development is perceived to be a process of finite steps. These steps are defined, followed, and measured. All improvements are aimed at improving the process in one way or another. Six Sigma specialists add improvement steps, lean advocates systematically find and eliminate wasteful steps, design automation people automate steps. In other words, all improvement initiatives will always be based on that perception of a defined series of steps.

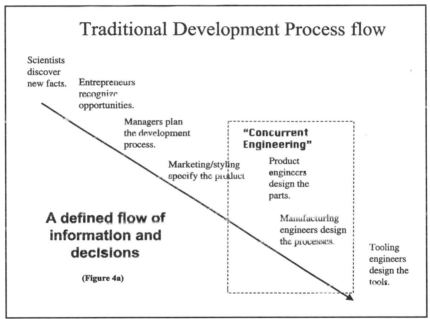

"This chart (Figure 4a) represents the typical process model for product development that basically fits all of the consortium companies. The model indicates more of a concurrent product and manufacturing design than most of the project companies really accomplish, but it is relatively accurate."

She looked from one team member to another. "Would you all agree this represents our company's view of a good product development process?"

Dick replied, "Largely. In fact, it's very close to the second layer process diagram we created yesterday, right?"

I agreed, pulled out that slide (Figure 3f) and put it back up.

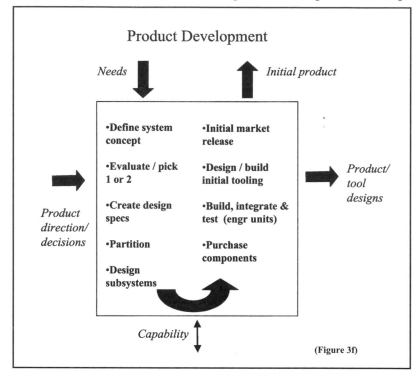

(Figure 3f)

Jan studied it for a few seconds. "There you are. They're basically the same. I'm hoping to get you to challenge this approach, and the assumptions that go with it, many of which stem from this paradigm." I could see her confidence growing as she pushed on. "Now, let's talk about what really happens on a project. We make a proposal that includes a conceptual view of the product and a rather detailed task-based schedule on how to accomplish the task of creating it. We follow this plan until it fails for whatever reason, then we follow a sequential series of iterative loop-backs, or plan modifications and resource changes, until the product design finally makes it to manufacturing. I won't take time to go into those problems. But I think you'll all agree we seem always to be late and over-budget, and even worse—with a sub-optimized solution."

Dick said, "Okay, I agree in general, but why do you say sub-optimized solution?"

Jan responded, "Because the original concept is never really challenged from the start of design until it fails. Oh, I'm sure that marketing kicked around some ideas during the fuzzy front end, but inevitably the proposal concept gets cast in stone. A task-based approach forces this because the schedule depends on stability from the start. As a result, many good ideas have to be set aside for early schedule efficiency."

Tim broke in. "Are you telling us, Jan, that another way to do product development exists? I've been around this business for a while now, and I've never seen anything fundamentally different."

"Yes, that's just what I'm saying. Our NCMS project struggled hard with that issue for months. Bear with me for a few minutes and I think you'll see."

Greg said, "Jan, you've just addressed some of the fundamental issues raised yesterday. Are you going to show us another approach?"

"Yes, I am, but I'd like to back up first to give you some more background. Is that okay?"

Tim seemed uncomfortable, but I nodded.

Jan said, "Let me just talk a few minutes about Toyota and also Nippondenso, their chief supplier."

Vijay added, "And also a potential competitor with us in the automotive IR business."

Jan nodded and continued. "Toyota and Denso are much faster than their competition, up to twice as fast. Toyota has never missed a launch date, nor do they miss interim milestones. And they consistently have the best quality in the industry. Denso has never had a U.S. recall. This is partly due to the fact that they have a very high reuse of both designs and manufacturing systems."

Dennis interrupted her. "That's interesting. Do they have a reuse strategy? That was one of our issues."

"No they don't" she said, "but I'm glad you asked. That's something that has bugged me about this company for years.

Everybody else in the world reuses stuff that works. Cooks reuse recipes, even hand them down through generations. Football teams replicate plays that work. Manufacturing sets standards to ensure reuse. Yet in traditional product development, we can't even define a strategy to effectively pull what appears to happen naturally everywhere else. Toyota doesn't have a formal strategy. Rather, it's fundamental to the Toyota operating philosophy. You'll see what I mean in a few minutes."

As she moved ahead I could see that most of our team were slowly gaining confidence in her.

She continued, "And they are also more productive. Toyota has more car launches per year than any other company. They also use one-quarter the number of engineers that U.S. companies have on a car project. Our study indicated they have about eighty percent value-added labor with their engineers. Even a senior manager at Toyota reported ninety percent value-added for his labor. I think you'll agree these are pretty amazing numbers."

I said, "Wait a minute. Did you say that Toyota engineers have eighty percent value-added productivity against what we described yesterday as twenty percent here? Are we talking about the same metric?"

"Yes and yes," Jan replied. "In our project meetings, we had a lot of discussion about that. It seems that all of our companies had similarly low numbers and we were all consistent in our definitions. Also, the number of engineers at Toyota compared to other companies bears this out."

Tim frowned. "Jan, I find that hard to believe. How can one company be that much more efficient?"

"One thing is certain," Jan said. "It can't be done simply by streamlining tasks. That's why we needed to get above that perspective."

Lori observed that Jan had hit on most of our issues from yesterday. I believe all of us, except maybe Tim, were in agreement that Toyota seemed to have a fundamentally better development environment than ours.

Jan concluded this part of her discussion by asking, "Did I make my case about Toyota being an exceptional company?"

Tim shook his head. "How about Toyota versus other Japanese companies? You seem to only compare them to ours."

"From what we learned, the same comparison holds up with one exception. Honda seems to have similar results and philosophies. Even so, Toyota is pretty unique in how it works. Lean manufacturing was also inspired by the Toyota production system—but it, too, is totally different from the company's product development process."

So much of what Jan had said was consistent with my thoughts that I was getting pretty excited to hear the rest of the story. I called for a fifteen-minute break.

During the break, I reflected on what Jan had said so far. Toyota was obviously on a different performance level than its competitors. The company didn't seem to have the fundamental issues we'd discussed yesterday. But it was difficult to grasp why and that made me uncomfortable. I wanted to see a side-by-side process chart to help me understand the differences. Then it dawned on me that it wouldn't be that easy. Toyota didn't approach product development as a process. It was clear the challenge was to step outside the box and begin to think of product development in a whole new way.

The break ended and Jan took the floor again.

"Let me talk about our project," she began. "We really struggled on how best to understand and attack the problem. Most of the initiatives at the consortium companies had changed from improvement at the functional level to improvement at the process level, but none had been successful in achieving major gains. Our consortium spent a considerable amount of time comparing product development process documentation from a number of good companies. We understood the processes. We could critique them. And we jointly enhanced them. But we knew we were just rearranging deck chairs on the Titanic. There were no revelations." She paused and looked at me. "I realize IRT is very proud of the PDSP standard process, but really, it is nothing special when compared to what exists at other companies. The processes might be packaged differently, maybe even have some clever differences, but there is nothing earth shaking."

Her eyes moved from one person to the next. "When Dr. Ward started presenting the Toyota environment, we were lost. We couldn't see the process. The truth is, the whole thing seemed chaotic. It was a totally different paradigm. Dr. Ward was frustrated with us because we simply didn't understand. And we were frustrated because he wouldn't, or couldn't, describe Toyota in terms of a process view we could clearly see." She paused, perhaps to frame her thoughts. "It took us awhile, but we finally understood that we had to break out of the process paradigm if we were ever going to understand. Then we started making headway." She took a breath. "Let me say this. As we move ahead, try not to think of product development as a series of steps that result in a product, but rather as an overall environment that produces a stream of products."

Some expressed concern that the process would have to go in order to move toward the Toyota system, but in general, everyone seemed okay with what she was saying. I certainly was. Deep down I knew we had to do more than just improve what we already had in order to meet Jack's challenge.

Jan continued by putting up a slide on corporate capabilities (Figure 4b).

She said, "Our consortium struggled a lot about which paradigms we should focus on. We knew we had to find a model that would allow the differences to be understood between our company's methods and Toyota's. We finally settled on these characteristics as being the primary drivers for product development excellence." She pointed to the lists on her slide.

"We organized them by process, organization, and culture. We felt that significant variances existed from one company to the next concerning how they thought about each of these capabilities. These became their paradigms. Our goal was to find great companies, understand their paradigms for each of these capabilities, and then to adapt them to our companies. Still with me?"

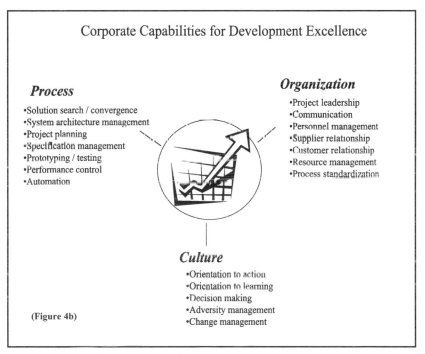

Corporate Capabilities for Development Excellence

Process
- Solution search / convergence
- System architecture management
- Project planning
- Specification management
- Prototyping / testing
- Performance control
- Automation

Organization
- Project leadership
- Communication
- Personnel management
- Supplier relationship
- Customer relationship
- Resource management
- Process standardization

Culture
- Orientation to action
- Orientation to learning
- Decision making
- Adversity management
- Change management

(Figure 4b)

She received understanding nods and continued. "Most of the capabilities are pretty obvious, but I might comment on a few that might not be. 'Solution search and convergence' is how a company decides on the product direction, or features, and how it converges on the final solution. Remember, I'm talking about the approach or paradigm, not the specific process steps. 'Orientation to learning' and 'Orientation to action' are interesting cultural capabilities. We believe that companies whose employees are much better at learning and motivated to get things done will be more successful." She paused. "Any comments before I move on?"

Facing a combination of nods and confused looks, Jan plunged ahead. "We then created three matrices—one each for process, organization, and culture—that define the different paradigms for each of these characteristics. This allowed us to see differences between the operational paradigms of the companies beyond simply the process steps. I made copies and will pass them out later so you can see the details." (See Appendix B for details of the NCMS project and complete matrices.)

Tim shifted in his chair and stuck up a hand. "When do you start comparing us to Toyota?"

Jan chuckled. "Actually, right now I just wanted you to get a flavor of the process we went through and the concept of product development paradigms. In reality, most of our companies were very similar in the paradigms they used for each of the capabilities. Toyota was different almost right down the list. Let me just speak to some of the key differences. But let me caution you, and this is very important, don't think you can follow the simple change model of identifying and removing the gaps between the current state and the desired state. For example, in manufacturing, improving the efficiency of managing in-house inventory would be useless in a just-in-time environment since inventory doesn't exist. Likewise, improving drawing control would be meaningless in a fully CAD database environment."

Glancing back at the process matrix, Jan continued. "Starting with 'Solution search / convergence', at IRT, as in most companies, we use 'requirements flow down' as the fundamental paradigm for converging on the solution. Customer requirements are defined early, followed by more detailed design and interface specifications as the process moves forward. Toyota is different. They don't do things this way. In fact, this may be the most fundamental difference. They build sets of possibilities to satisfy their customer's needs, and through a series of combining and narrowing they arrive at the solution."

Dick suddenly blurted out, "Jan, what the hell are you talking about? Am I the only one who has no idea what you just said?

You mean Toyota doesn't have defined specifications?"

"They do, but they aren't finalized until the end of the process," Jan said. "At Toyota, specifications are the documentation of the results, not a recipe of the plan. As I said, it's a different paradigm. Frankly, I'd rather not go into more detail before getting all the paradigms on the table."

"Go ahead then. But Jon, I'm not at all comfortable with all this. It seems too academic to be real."

Dick was putting it on the record, which Greg was keeping on his laptop, that he was not on board. I could tell that a number of others felt the same. Still, I motioned for Jan to continue. I could tell she was getting a little defensive. She was sharp, but this was a tough crowd for a young engineer to face.

She continued down the list of process capabilities. "In the interest of time, I really don't want to go into the details of each Toyota paradigm. Certainly not just yet. I'll just summarize each type of capability so you can get a feel for how different the people at Toyota think in their approach to product development. If you want to get into more detail, we can do that later. But the detail is meaningless until you understand the paradigm."

I nodded approval. I must admit that I did not understand how Toyota operated, but I was afraid we'd lose the forest for the trees if we took time to analyze details at this point.

Jan continued. "Toyota will designate a chief engineer who is totally responsible for all aspects of a product. It's his car, period. Even so, the people who help him don't report to him. He's the best engineer on the project. He makes technical decisions. He teaches and manages by continually asking 'why.' He reviews status through prototypes and analyses, not completed tasks. Other car companies call their administrative managers 'chief engineers.' We call ours 'program managers.' The names are similar. The paradigm is different." Jan took a breath. "Another difference is in how they do planning and control. They don't use project-wide task-time based planning systems like we do. They decentralize the planning in that the people doing the work are responsible."

I could sense uneasiness growing in the room, but thought it best to get an overview of the differences on the table. I could tell Jan was getting more and more uncomfortable as she sensed the mood of the team. So I said, "Keep going, Jan. You're doing great."

"As I mentioned earlier," she said, "Toyota's design specs emerge throughout the process and are not the focal points for information handoffs. In terms of prototyping and testing, our method is to do as little as possible for verification. Toyota does lots of prototyping but primarily to gain 'live' knowledge required for decision making. The responsibility for project performance is at the individual level—it's not that of the organization. Lastly, Toyota does not focus on CAD/CAM design automation as a critical part of their product development process. As you know, we use ours to help enforce process standards. I know you're not comfortable with your level of understanding of Toyota's system at this point, but I hope you understand how differently we look at product development than they do."

Switching to the organizational matrix, Jan continued. "On the organizational side, the differences seem subtler than in the process paradigm. But in some cases they are actually more revealing. It seems that everything we do in terms of organizational setup is to provide effective administration of policies and procedures whereas everything Toyota does is to provide technical leadership. We charter and co-locate teams to force better cross-functional communication. Communication is not forced at Toyota. It's simply a natural result of the environment. We add structure to force individual behavior. It just happens at Toyota. Their organizational behavior is required to support their process paradigms. The job of the leaders is to pull the technical knowledge from the people. At IRT, new engineers know that they need to move into management as soon as possible to be on the fast-track. We know we actually get raises on the basis of our management potential. Poorer engineers who present well are perceived as being more valuable than excellent engineers. This is the primary reason I'm looking outside." She stopped herself. "Pardon me for getting personal. Even the way we manage our suppliers is from an administrative perspective. They work to our hard specifications. Toyota has full partnering with its suppliers. Obviously, they have fewer suppliers that they work with."

Dennis said, "Our purchasing improvement team has been struggling with how to reduce our supplier base and get them more involved within the process. We've not made much headway except for management lip service."

I said, "Maybe that's the fundamental problem, Dennis. Your team is trying to push a solution inconsistent with the current paradigm—whereas at Toyota, the solution is pulled by the way they operate."

Tim said, "C'mon, Jon, you're not buying into all of this, are you? All this is much too philosophical. I see no base to build from."

I could see that Dick agreed with him. Everyone else seemed intrigued but searching for something to focus on. At IRT, program managers were generally pretty aggressive and would often bully their way in meetings. That's why they disliked Troy. He never became intimidated and could yell louder than anyone.

"Tim," I said in a harsh tone, "it's okay by me to cover some organizational philosophy. Frankly, as far as I'm concerned, a lot of this makes sense. Of course, I can't say I've figured out how to apply it. But let's just let it play out for a while." I looked at Jan. "Go ahead. Your show." I wasn't about to be bullied and was indeed buying into the philosophy and potential—even though I hadn't yet grasped a starting point for change.

Jan said, "My last comment concerning this matrix is that IRT insists on imposing a standard process—whereas, at Toyota, it's much looser. Their people are expected to know what to do."

She then pointed to the cultural matrix. "The cultural paradigms are the ones that focus on how the people think. I only want to address the top two. 'Orientation to action' is what motivates the workforce. At IRT and companies like ours, people are motivated to impress their bosses. We called that the 'advocate' paradigm because the people feel their future is decided by who they impress. If you took a poll of our engineers, I'm sure they'd agree that being proficient in PowerPoint is more important than their CAD capability. At Toyota, the engineer is motivated only to be an excellent product design engineer.

"The next capability 'orientation to learning' addresses how technical knowledge is shared. Here we have models of how things are done and a few experts who are responsible for those models. Our PDSP Process is an example. At Toyota, all individuals are expected to learn what works and what doesn't. They don't have procedures on how to do things. They have documentation on actual design results which everyone has access to and is expected to use. The engineers are measured on how well they contribute to and use these design 'checklists.'" She looked at me. "Jon, I think I've gone as far as I need to on this."

Tim came at Jan again. "Jan, are you trying to tell us we need to make all those paradigm shifts to solve our problems? If so, I can't agree you've made your case. Besides, even if we wanted to, you haven't given us a single hint on how to do it."

Jan said, "Tim, I'm not telling you we need to do anything. I'm telling you that Toyota has an outstanding, maybe the best, product development process anywhere. Don't kill the messenger. I'm just reporting that they have a significantly different product development paradigm. Trying to mimic any part of Toyota's development system without understanding their underlying design philosophies would be a mistake. I've a few more slides that show how our NCMS project pulled it all together. I think I can finish in about 30 minutes. Is that okay? That will take us to about lunchtime."

I said, "Go ahead, Jan, I agree we need to understand this."

Jan said, "The fact that Toyota seemed to be diametrically opposed to IRT and other companies on almost every paradigm caused us to look for an overriding top-level paradigm that could explain the wide dichotomy. We decided there was a simpler way to view the differences—that what a company values in effect pulls operational paradigms accordingly. It seemed rather easy for us to define and characterize two high-level paradigms that seemed to illustrate the two different philosophies."

This seemed logical. Trying to make operational changes without first establishing a top-level philosophy or vision would be virtually impossible. The difference appeared to be that it's far easier to pull correct behavior from people than it is to push it on them. In manufacturing, when we started thinking lean, we started acting lean. Many of the lean concepts had actually been attempted earlier and had largely failed. My sculpture analogy again came to mind—if you don't have a clear picture of the end result, how are you going to get there?

Jan put up a slide which defined two new paradigms, *Structure-based* and *Knowledge-based* (Figure 4c).

Development Environment Extremes

A Continuum

Structure-Based	Knowledge-Based
The basis of the engineering environment is the *structure of the operational activities*: procedures, control, compliance, related training **(Figure 4c)**	The basis of the engineering environment is the *knowledge of individual workers*: understanding of needs, information availability, responsibility, and teaming interaction

---

"If you look at our operational paradigms on the earlier Process, Organization, and Culture charts, they're all structural.

IRT and most companies have an engineering environment based on procedures, control, and compliance. Toyota's paradigms are based on the knowledge possessed by the individual worker. This is what leads to their success. These two ways of looking at product development are fundamentally different. One values organizational structure. The other values individual knowledge. The operational paradigms are pulled accordingly."

Jan put up her attributes slide (Figure 4d).

Development Environment Attributes

Attributes	*Structural*	*Knowledge*
Operational Focus	Planning & Control	Doing & Learning
Progress Evaluation	Task Completions	Direct Observations
Basis for Personal Reward	Compliance	Knowledge / Expertise
Improvement Focus	Task Efficiency	Learning Efficiency

(Figure 4d)

"These are some attributes that will be pulled once a company establishes that top level philosophy or paradigm. This is an important comparison. Let me walk you through it. The operational focus of a structural environment is clearly on a planning and control paradigm, where Toyota, and the knowledge-based environment, emphasizes doing and learning. The structural paradigm measures progress by how many tasks are complete. In a knowledge-based paradigm, you would directly observe results. Design reviews are based on product prototypes and analysis, not words. Likewise, in a structural environment, business metrics are operations based, like the number of drawings completed, as opposed to knowledge, such as Design for Six Sigma analysis. The basis for personal rewards is compliance to the process rather than knowledge or achievement, and the improvement focus is on the efficiency of process tasks rather than learning efficiency. I believe that IRT is best characterized by the left side of the chart, and that the right side is clearly a more desirable environment.

Looking around the room, I could see that Jan had everyone intrigued. I saw that even Dick and Tim seemed to agree in principle—to a degree at least.

To me, philosophically, it looked good, but then so did a water mirage to a desert wanderer. I decided to push the issue. "In my opinion we won the National Quality Award because we had strong procedures on almost everything and could prove we followed them. If I'm to believe Jan's argument, then the fundamental premise of that award is flawed because it is actually encouraging unproductive behavior. Also, it would seem that the Six Sigma Initiative, which is largely a philosophy of customer-based thinking, is misused when it's executed primarily through a series of internal metrics and procedures. It seems to me that's what we do when we try to apply defect measurements on activities that don't impact the customer but rather, impact internal procedures."

The looks on faces around the room reflected a strange mixture of excitement that we might be on to something, intrigue as to what it was, and confusion as to what to do or say next. I think we all knew that whatever it was couldn't be ignored.

Tim spoke up. "Jan, you really did a nice job and your project was well done. But I find it disheartening to think we can only get to product development nirvana by changing ourselves to look like Toyota, or by being knowledge-based. I feel like I've been on a wagon train heading to California for two months, and now you're telling me to turn around and head for Florida. And even worse, as best I could tell, you didn't give me a map to Florida. You just told me I'd like it when I got there. It's not realistic."

I laughed. "But what if I can convince you that you'll never make it to California because wild Indians are waiting over the next hill. And besides, I have a nice lot on a golf course waiting for you in Florida." I shook my head. "How much money we've spent to get where we are shouldn't be a factor. We're losing the race, Tim." I turned to Jan. "Anything else before we break for lunch?"

"Yes," Jan said. "Let me wrap it up with a slightly different way of looking at the differences, but more from a process perspective. When I began today, I showed you a slide on the point-based process. We agreed it was similar to our process. That was a structural-based process view. This one (Figure 4e) is the knowledge-based view. In effect, the product emerges from the interaction of the collective knowledge of all perspectives. In my

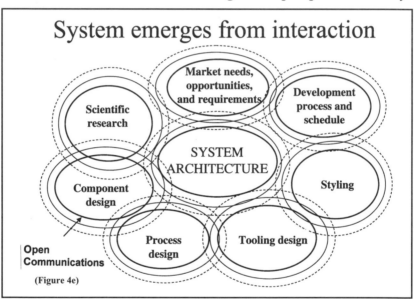

After looking at this, we broke for lunch.

It was interesting that at lunch our discussion didn't center around our project. I think Jan overwhelmed us with more information than we could assimilate. Tim and Dick hadn't joined us. I was concerned we were becoming fragmented. Indeed, when we got back to the room, Dick asked if he could have a few minutes to discuss a concern he and Tim had. Obviously, they'd been working over lunch.

"Tim and I tried to think through issues over lunch. We believe that Jan and her NCMS project did an excellent job of characterizing a fundamentally better environment than we have. But that doesn't mean it can be implemented here. We've tried to understand the essence of the change required. Jan, your first and last charts were a view of the point-based process and the knowledge-based view—I think it was labeled 'emergence.' Correct?"

"Yes, basically," Jan said.

Dick continued. "We also agreed that the point-based process was the same as the high-level view of our process. If this is so, then I can show that the change that you're asking us to make is like the following chart." He put a new chart up that defined his perspective of the process change required (Figure 4f).

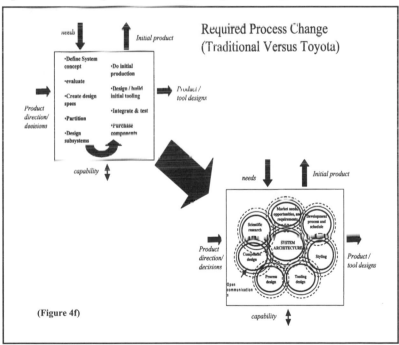

(Figure 4f)

After leaving up the chart for a few moments, Dick began. "Unless we're mistaken, this is a fifty-thousand-foot view of the essence of the change we're talking about. Our process, on the left, is a defined flow of activities that start with requirements and end with a product delivered to the customer. Correct?"

After mostly non-disagreeing blank stares, he continued. "And on the right is Toyota, where somehow knowledge flows rampantly throughout all organizations—and cars, great cars, just keep emerging like clockwork. WOW! A really big WOW!" Dick stopped talking and looked around the room.

Jan began to speak, "Well, let me—"

Dick cut her off. "Jan, now please don't get defensive. I'm not saying it isn't right, and I'm certainly not attacking you. I think you've done a great job, and I think we all really appreciate what you've told us, and that you took the time to do so—but let me continue . . . "

Before he could, everyone chimed in to thank Jan. She seemed to appreciate it, and relaxed back in her chair.

Dick continued. "Our issue is whether we know enough about how they do it to consider recommending it. Do we really understand enough details to even know how to begin? Per the agenda, we're supposed to be generating ideas. We have one that's way out there . . . great food for thought, but is it ready for primetime? Before we spend more time on it, Tim and I think we should table it and focus on generating some new ideas that are hopefully less dramatic in their implications."

I had to admit he had a point, but I also knew we couldn't just drop it. It represented too much potential gain. Had any company ever actually made such a transformation? Was there any evidence outside of Toyota that this approach was really that effective? I needed to be careful not to overreact to the first idea that actually showed promise. On the other hand, much of what Jan had said seemed to sit well in my gut. Usually, my first reaction had proven to be correct.

"Jan, do you have more detail on any of this?" I asked.

"Kind of," she said. "I mentioned Dr. Allen Ward. He's the guru when it comes to adapting Toyota's approach for American industry. In our NCMS project we tried to widen the search, but we didn't find anything. Allen has given a number of workshops in connection with our project and on his own that offer more detail about the Toyota principles. He calls it the Lean Product Development process, as opposed to Knowledge-based. I think he does so because he's such a proponent of lean manufacturing. Anyway, I've a number of his slides I could pull together."

"Could you do that by tomorrow morning?"

"Sure," she said with a laugh. "That is, if Jack calls and asks."

Tim spoke up in a frustrated tone. "Damn it, Jon, why do you keep pushing this so hard?"

I could feel my face flush. "Because we have twenty percent value-added labor and Toyota has eighty. I realize that we don't know enough of the details at this point, but the potential is just too exciting. Why not let it play out?" I looked from Tim to the others. "The floor is now open for other new ideas." I shifted my glance back to Tim. "Show me anything with similar potential benefits and I'll stop pushing. I refuse to accept that this company can't dramatically change." I turned to Jan. "Can you get me the phone number for Dr. Ward?"

"Sure," she said. "I'll leave it with your secretary. Allen will be glad to talk to you, but remember, he's from academia."

I didn't know whether she meant her last comment as a complement to Allen or a warning to me. Oh, well.

"All right," I said, "let's talk about other ideas for major gains in product development. But let me warn everyone, I'll veto any approach that adds more structure to our environment."

Jan excused herself to go get her slides ready. For the next two hours we kicked around lots of ideas, but none that had any potential for major improvement. We considered more automation, a new Six Sigma strategy, a new teaming strategy, but nothing that had any serious potential for making dramatic improvements. Finally, I dismissed the meeting and asked everyone to think about it for the next morning.

It was only about three o'clock when I arrived back at my office, but I was beat.

Donna poked her head in. "Welcome back," she said, then slipped all the way in and sat down. "Not going well?" Her eyebrows were raised in a question. I braced myself for a pep talk.

"How could you tell?"

"I can read you like a book."

I decided to brief her. I knew she wouldn't leave until I did. "We brought this engineer in today to brief us on a consortium project. She convinced us we were all screwed up. Then we convinced ourselves that we probably couldn't do anything about it."

"Jan, right? She left a phone number for you. I put it on your note pad. Attractive, right?"

I felt my eyebrows lift. "Well, yes, but how did you guess that and what difference does it make?"

Smiling, she said, "It makes no difference. It's just that you always do something funny with your eyebrows when you see or talk about an attractive woman."

I felt myself blush. "I do not."

"Hey, I'm just trying to keep you out of trouble," she said. Sometimes this woman could drive me crazy, but I wondered if that was why my wife punched me so often in a shopping mall. Anyway, I debriefed her on the Toyota approach and change issues.

She listened for a while, then said, "Let me tell you a story that might help."

"I'm listening." I kidded her a lot, but she had always been insightful and always seemed to be right.

"You know that cooking is a passion with me."

I nodded, thinking that was an understatement. Donna had become famous for her cooking skills and had even had her own cookbook published for a local charity. She periodically gave dinner parties that were unbelievable.

She continued. "Well, I was going through my attic the other day and came across my old cookbooks from when I was just learning. For years I just collected recipes and followed instructions exactly. That got boring, so I decided I wanted to start creating my own. Luckily, my grandmother was an incredible cook, as was my mother-in-law, so I started asking them more and more questions. I started my own notebook, which didn't have exact recipes, but was more about what worked and what didn't work. I still use that today, but haven't looked at any of those old recipe books for years. Now all my energy is spent on creating new things. I never have a dinner party that isn't different from before."

"You're kidding," I replied. "Every time you create a new dinner—that's like a new product."

"So why do you think I'm bringing this up?" She shook her head. "I'm not trying to give you a cooking lesson. Anyway, I never totally do a new dinner, just parts of it. I start with some sort of theme, then I put together sets of things that I think will work—wine, salads, meat, vegetables, and so on. Then I combine stuff and maybe focus on one thing—sauce, dessert, or whatever to make it unique. After the party, I make notations in my notebook about the results based on comments or what wasn't eaten. Seems to me I moved from a structural environment to a knowledge environment when I tossed all my cookbooks and started building from my own expertise. That's what your good-looking lady engineer was trying to say, and you decided it wasn't possible. It seems to me maybe you just need to allow your engineers to be good engineers."

Having dumped that on me, she got up and left.

I spent a while in my office thinking about what she'd said. My frustration level was high, and I couldn't put my finger on why. Jan had given a logical explanation of how Toyota achieved an amazing 80% productivity—a number that would more than satisfy Jack's demand to turn this company around. I was convinced that if we could achieve that metric, all other performance metrics would be excellent. I finally decided my frustration came from the fact that I didn't know enough about the change required to make that leap, or how to accomplish the change even if I did know.

On a whim, I tried to write a short vision statement on what I'd learned:

The Vision is for IRT to develop a product development environment that focuses on capturing, disseminating, and orchestrating product knowledge to create an ongoing stream of products.

How powerful would it be if every piece of knowledge—what had worked and what hadn't at all levels of design—was available to every engineer doing development? This was what Jan was saying. The challenge was both exciting and bewildering. How in the hell had Toyota achieved this, and how long had it taken? I was afraid the answer was that they'd started there. I wasn't sure I'd survive Jack's stare if I told him we'd evolve to Toyota's level over the next 50 years.

I needed to think, so I decided to go to the driving range. My gut feeling was that we were onto something here, but I had nothing substantive to back it up. It was not in my nature to make uninformed decisions—although I believed that my intuition had been proven correct more often than not.

As I walked through the parking lot, I listed issues in my mind:
- I firmly believe our current environment and initiatives will not resolve our problems.
- The Toyota principles are logical and intuitive.
- Can a North American company really make such a transformation, or is it an inbred cultural thing?
- What happens if we only get part way?
- What will it take for me to make this recommendation?

I decided to call this Dr. Ward.

DISCUSSION

This chapter proposed a new product development paradigm, Knowledge-based Development, as the vision for excellence in product development. From a change perspective, this typically would have been one of many possibilities explored for resolving the fundamental issues. In the IRT example, I alluded to other options, but concentrated on the knowledge-based paradigm. Ideally, each of the possibilities would be refined and tested for viability and results, and a vision would emerge from this.

When exploring the possibilities, the following should be kept in mind as important to following a good change process.

1. Tap the knowledge of the workforce.

My experience has been that a vast amount of knowledge, experience, and creativity exists within a company. What's needed is for someone to listen. The problem is not that management doesn't want to. In general, it simply doesn't have the right context in which to listen. Employees often have innovative ideas about improving their local work environment, but no way of integrating them with other good ideas in order to create a better overall process. This is the challenge of the change process.

In this case study, a team of experts from across the product development environment was called on to develop a new vision for the company. In my experience, many improvement teams come and go at companies, but few actually contain people who are the real experts or are genuinely chartered to make changes.

The bottom line is that any serious change effort at a company must involve the true internal experts as active and responsible participants in the process.

2. Balance the level of detail with understanding.

In exploring possibilities for change, the level of detail must be sufficient for understanding, but it must not be allowed to become so overwhelming that it buries the philosophical logic. Too much detail on any possibility can stifle creativity. Sufficient detail must exist, however, for analysis of benefits versus risk. The next step in the change process is to narrow the possibilities and to begin the transformation of the vision into reality. The change leader must balance the details.

In our case study, consensus exists concerning the probable benefits of the knowledge-based environment. But legitimate concern runs deep about the practical viability of it. More detail is required for full evaluation, which leads us to the next chapter.

Chapter 5

Transforming the Vision
(The Power of the System)

A new operational vision is one thing; transferring that vision into system reality is much more difficult. It requires challenging, and often changing, long-held procedures, tools, and policies. These changes must appear logical and workable to the workforce and be fully supported by management.

Friday morning, Infrared Technologies Corporation

At least there was not much traffic on the way in. I had a lot to think through. Jack had called the previous night to let me know the management meeting was set for Monday morning at nine. That meant I had only today to finish getting input from the team. I didn't want to work with them on Saturday. I needed the weekend to put my slides together. Jack reiterated that we should be bold. Unfortunately, he didn't have time for me to discuss the issues we were struggling with. Also, I'd tried to reach Dr. Ward, but all I got was his answering machine.

As I cruised along I thought about Donna's cooking analogy. It definitely intrigued me. Yesterday, Jan had brought up sets of possibilities when discussing one of Toyota's paradigms. It was interesting that Donna had actually used the same terms when she had discussed how she invented new recipes. In fact, many of her comments seemed consistent with the Toyota concepts. Maybe, just maybe, we were the ones who'd screwed up what's really the natural product development process—as opposed to Toyota

117

having invented a new paradigm. It seemed like we put so much energy into proceduralizing improvements like concurrent engineering and Six Sigma. Toyota appeared to have personalized the concepts within the individual engineers. Even so, making such a change would be extremely difficult. It was important to get Tim and Dick on board. With a chuckle I wondered what would happen if I brought Troy in to sit between them.

It's amazing how many things Jan brought up about Toyota that made such clear sense. I was itching to move ahead, but needed the team to agree.

I hoped that Jan was ready. Hell, I hoped Dick and Tim just showed up.

The drive was too short to sort all of this out.

I didn't see Troy when I stopped by the cafeteria. My bet was he was on the golf course. We were finally getting some warm weather. I wondered whether that was where I'd rather be as I approached the conference room.

Everyone was there. This was the most on-time group I'd ever seen. They were looking at their watches as if I was late. Actually, I was two minutes early. Everyone seemed to be in a relatively good mood—even Tim and Jan were having a civil conversation.

I stood at the head of the table. "Okay, are we ready to start? I talked to Jack last night. The meeting is nine o'clock on Monday. You're all invited. It will be only us and the leadership team."

"Does that include me?" Jan asked. "I realize I'm not an official team member."

"Absolutely," I said. "Jack wants to meet you."

Jan smiled. "Oh, great. I wonder what I said to him the other night. But thanks for inviting me."

Lori spoke. "Jon, I'm on vacation next week. What's the plan for more meetings?"

"I honestly don't know. If we're successful at least to some degree, I assume there will be some follow-up."

Lori said, "Can I send Robin Liebermann to the meeting to represent me next week?"

"Sure," I said, even though I really didn't want to get anyone else involved at this point. "Before Jan takes us deeper into the world of Toyota, let's talk about any other new ideas or approaches. Anybody?" I hoped we didn't get totally derailed.

Tim took the lead. "Jon, I really tried to come up with something, but I just kept coming back to variations on what we are already doing, and I know that's not what you're looking for. I'm still concerned about the Toyota approach. It's interesting, but really has no meat to it. Nothing we can sink our teeth into. You have to be there, at Toyota, to make it work." He shook his head. "I'm glad you're the one who has to present."

Carl added, "The only thing I can think of is to redesign the PDSP process to simplify it and add some of these new ideas. But frankly, I think that's a Band-Aid. The fact that Toyota is four times more productive than us certainly makes a case for continuing on the Toyota bandwagon. The problem is adapting it to the way we think."

After about 30 more minutes of discussion, we all agreed that our current improvement initiatives, Six Sigma, the PDSP standard process, and design automation, were not going to resolve our issues, and that philosophically, at least, the knowledge-based approach was our best bet. I turned the meeting back to Jan, hoping she could pull some magic out of her hat.

She stood. "Okay, is everyone going to be nice to me today?" Jan seemed more comfortable today as she walked to the head of the table and turned on the overhead projector. "I put together a number of slides that illustrate the Toyota approach in more detail. As I mentioned yesterday, a lot of this material is based on the work of Dr. Allen Ward and workshops I attended. He worked for a number of years while a professor at the University of Michigan to understand and apply the Toyota process to American industry, and was a consultant to our NCMS project.

Allen calls the system 'Lean Product Development,' but it's the same as 'Knowledge-based,' as we discussed yesterday. He focuses a lot on eliminating waste. That's why he calls it lean. It's the elimination of waste that allows the productivity to be so much higher. I think you'll see as I go through the details that Knowledge-based product development concepts automatically eliminate waste. Personally, I like the name 'Knowledge-based' better than 'Lean Development.' It seems more illustrative to me and won't get confused with lean manufacturing."

I said, "I assume that any activity that doesn't build on the knowledge needed to develop a product can be considered waste or non-value-added—from the perspective of the end customer."

"Yes," Jan said. "That's a fair statement—as long as you recognize that the knowledge that something didn't work is good."

"So long as you don't lose the knowledge," Carl said. "That would be waste."

Jan nodded and she put up her first slide (Figure 5a).

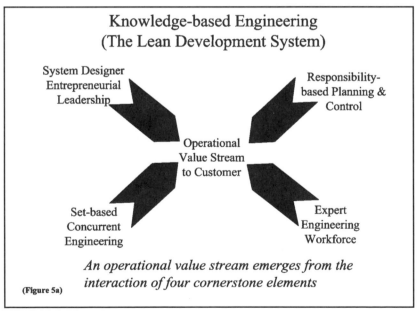

Knowledge-based Engineering
(The Lean Development System)

System Designer
Entrepreneurial
Leadership

Responsibility-
based Planning &
Control

Operational
Value Stream
to Customer

Set-based
Concurrent
Engineering

Expert
Engineering
Workforce

An operational value stream emerges from the interaction of four cornerstone elements

(Figure 5a)

"This is a conceptual view of the Knowledge-based Development System, or Lean Development System, that shows the critical elements. I'll cover each one in detail. The goal of the system is to generate a consistent value stream to the customer. It's more than just developing a single product. It has to support manufacturing operations in keeping a consistent flow of product through the factory."

Dick interrupted. "Jan, I like that wording. I think it means that scheduling slippages cannot be allowed, and that has to go beyond manufacturing. We can't plan resources with slippages."

Jan seemed genuinely pleased that one of her adversaries from yesterday had something positive to say. So was I.

Then Jay asked a question I'd been struggling with. "How do these four relate to the ones in your matrices that we discussed yesterday?"

"Actually, these are the four from yesterday," Jan said. "Remember, our NCMS project was focused on defining new paradigms. What I'm presenting here is the view from an implementation perspective. We believe that if a company implements these four critical capabilities, the rest of the capabilities and the right paradigms will be pulled."

Tim said, "In other words, in theory we simply need to focus on these to make it all work." He sounded apprehensive.

"That's the theory," Jan said. "The logic is simple. Set-based concurrent engineering is the process for searching and converging on the solution. This will work only if the engineering workforce has the expertise to execute the demands of the set-based environment, if the project leadership has the technical background for decision-making, and if the project is planned and controlled through distributed responsibility. All of the resources must be aligned to make it work. When this is the case, we're convinced the product will emerge from the interaction."

Dennis said, "So what you're saying is that the implementation pillars are the process, the people, the leaders, and the control system. And all need to be aligned to the knowledge-based paradigm."

"That's correct," Jan said with confidence.

Tim asked, "Where are the suppliers in this scheme?"

"They're another organization that follows the same set-based process. Their input concerning the possibilities will be considered equally by the chief engineer. What's the logic in treating suppliers as adversaries and thinking they have to be tightly controlled?"

Jan waited to see if there were any more questions. Then she said, "Okay, let's talk about set-based concurrent engineering, but let's not over-think it." She was about to discuss what everybody had been wondering about since she brought it up yesterday, except apparently for Donna.

Jan put up a new slide (Figure 5b).

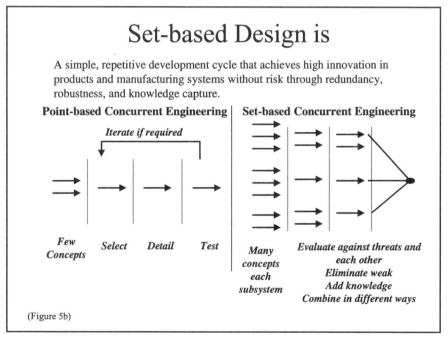

Set-based Design is

A simple, repetitive development cycle that achieves high innovation in products and manufacturing systems without risk through redundancy, robustness, and knowledge capture.

Point-based Concurrent Engineering | **Set-based Concurrent Engineering**

Iterate if required

Few Concepts   *Select*   *Detail*   *Test*

Many concepts each subsystem   *Evaluate against threats and each other*
Eliminate weak
Add knowledge
Combine in different ways

(Figure 5b)

"I have several slides that show the power of this process versus our point-based process. The left side of this one is a snapshot of the point-based process, which I think we all agree is what we do. In it you select one of a few system concepts, partition the design into subsystems through interface specifications, develop the subsystems independently, and then integrate it all at the system level. We all know the problems we generally have at the integration level, which invariably result in iterations that are unplanned and weave themselves through all the subsystems, causing all kinds of firefighting and confusion. In other words, our typical program." She took a breath. "Did I exaggerate?"

Lori said, "No, that's the way we typically do development and these 'loopbacks' were one of the primary issues we discussed on our first day, but I'd like to vent a bit about how bad it really is. The amount of waste caused is just awful. These changes are never planned, they ripple through all design teams, causing confusion and more errors while everyone tries to adjust, which causes more errors and more loopbacks. We really love it when you hardware guys decide you can't do it and hand it over to us in software, which screws up all of our architecture and plans. AAUUG!"

Nobody said anything for a few moments. I guess we were all shocked at the fervor coming from sweet, mild-mannered Lori.

Greg broke the silence, looked at Lori and said, "Now tell us what you really think. And don't hold back!"

"Sorry, I got carried away." Lori said meekly.

She blushed as we all laughed at her expense.

Jan said, "Jump in anytime, Lori, as long as you stay on my side. Now, the set-based process is fundamentally different." She pointed to the right side of the slide. "You explore multiple sets of possibilities at the subsystem level against broad targets, then systematically narrow and/or combine to tighter targets. The interfaces stay loose to allow flexibility. It's really pretty simple. The possibilities are generated from every perspective— software, hardware, suppliers, manufacturing, whatever. A very important part of this process is redundancy. A subsystem solution you know will work is always one of the possibilities. Over time the redundancies will be dropped as the knowledge and confidence of what will work grows. Does this make sense?"

Tim said, "Conceptually, I must admit it does. I've always

wanted redundancy in my designs for risk mitigation, but neither my schedule nor the budget ever seems to allow it. On my last project, I tried to co-develop a new detector assembly with some great new features along with a lower risk version. Jorgenson vetoed the co-development—told me to pick one. I picked the low-risk alternative because I felt it was safer for my career. Eventually, the functionality of the low risk detector proved to be unacceptable, and now, months later, we're developing the new design, with all kinds of confusion, lost time, and wasted effort."

Vijay jumped in. "And that's the point, Tim. Redundancy has got to be cheaper than the inevitable unplanned loopbacks. Right, Lori?"

"Right," Lori said, blushing again.

Jan said, "But the rest of the lean elements must be in place in order to support this concept. We'll talk about that in a few minutes. Does everyone understand the set-based process?"

"Actually," I replied, "I had this all explained to me yesterday by my secretary." It was amazing to see all the blank stares in the room. "She's a rather acclaimed chef. What you described is exactly how she prepares for a dinner party—broad themes, submenu possibilities, redundancy, combination. The party just emerges. She did say that she keeps lots of data on her results."

"Yes, absolutely," Jan said. "We're going to talk about that when we discuss workforce expertise. I'd like to meet this secretary." She continued, "Jon's example points out that set-based is really the natural process, but our structural processes don't allow it. Try to justify planned redundancy to our accountants. They'll never understand how designing a backup early on can save money in the long run." She shuffled through her slides. "Now, I want to go into some things that naturally occur from the set-based process. Jon's secretary mentioned data. If you're going to have multiple sets of possibilities, you have to have good information in order to evaluate and narrow those possibilities. I want to show you the power of that information."

She put up her next slide (Figure 5c).

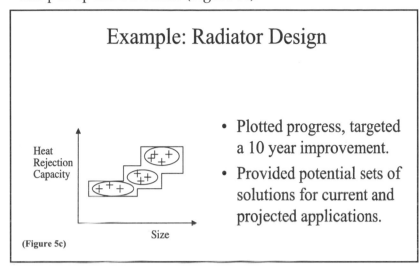

Example: Radiator Design

Heat Rejection Capacity

Size

(Figure 5c)

- Plotted progress, targeted a 10 year improvement.
- Provided potential sets of solutions for current and projected applications.

Jan pointed at the slide. "The plus signs on this chart are examples of data from different subsystem alternatives from a Toyota supplier for radiators. The key tradeoff data is the capacity versus size of the radiator. Toyota establishes these types of targets for all subsystems. This allows a supplier to plan long-range improvements based on how targets are changing, and it allows engineers on a specific project to develop sets of solutions that can be proposed for a particular new car model. Guess what happens to a design that doesn't make it into a specific car—maybe because the technology was not quite ready?"

I said, "Donna, my secretary, would answer that it goes into her data bank ready for the next dinner, or project."

"And she'd be correct," Jan replied, "resulting in a self-sustaining reuse and knowledge retention strategy. Sets of possibilities, rich in knowledge from prior projects, are always in waiting for the next project. Think how powerful this becomes when it's replicated across all car systems. Think of the power if this was replicated across all of our subsystems. Talk about a knowledge base."

Carl said, "Our systems engineering team has wrestled with a reuse strategy for years. What you're saying is that our point-

125

based process really doesn't demand that type of behavior."

Jan said, "No, it actually degrades it because all development is localized on entire projects not on common subsystems."

A perplexed look on her face, Lori said, "I'm not sure I understand that point. Can you explain what prevents us from capturing knowledge in our current system."

"Sure," Jan responded. "It isn't so much that we can't, but it's not natural for us to do so. As a result, knowledge will generally fall by the wayside. Let me explain. In our point-based process, subsystem designers design to system specs that encourage unique designs that are very difficult to categorize for sharing to other projects. At Toyota, subsystem performance data is the cornerstone for building the system design."

Lori still looked confused. She interrupted, "Jan, I have been struggling with Toyota's emphasis on tradeoff curves. Is this what we're talking about?"

"Yes, absolutely," Jan said. "The tradeoff curves provide the subsystem knowledge to create the system design, *and* to provide the ongoing knowledge for future projects. These curves are nothing more than the comparative mapping of the important subsystem design data to both system performance and other subsystem characteristics. I already mentioned radiators. The capability for heat removal is mapped versus size, weight, maybe cost, or even a Six Sigma rating. In our case, our detector assembly thermal sensitivity could be mapped against heat generation, size, and optical tolerances. By the way, most of this data is real data. That's why Toyota makes so many prototypes. These tradeoff curves are the cornerstone of knowledge. But please, don't get hung up on how these might actually look—just think of them as the technical standard for comparative knowledge."

Carl joined in. "So, based largely on the knowledge from these so called tradeoff curves, Toyota can build entirely new automobiles from proven subsystems—but wired together in different ways."

"That's correct," Jan said, "and I hope you see how redundancy plays in here allowing Toyota to have a risk adverse system balanced with the continual infusion of new ideas. Almost always, the subsystem designers will carry a proven subsystem as far as required to ensure that any new design is ready for primetime or can meet the changing system targets. Either way, the knowledge is not lost but is banked for the next project. Okay?"

Looking around the room, I could tell that everyone liked the concept but were struggling with envisioning how it might all work.

Switching gears, Jan put up her next slide (Figure 5d).

Learning to Effort Ratio

- Multiple subsystem alternatives explore more cheaply (allows platform projects)

- Expanded subsystem learning feeds knowledge back for future projects

3 bicycles

vs

3 frames

3 drives

3 wheel sets

3 brakes

3 suspensions
_____

= 243 combinations

(Figure 5d)

"How about 'learning to effort' ratio? Consider the design of three bicycles. If you design by multiple subsystem alternatives, you'll end up with many more combinations of designs than if you start with only a few entire system concepts. In point-based systems, you'd have only three unique bicycle designs. In set-based design, using three interchangeable sets of each subsystem, you could have 243 unique bicycles, resulting in significantly more knowledge when controlled at the subsystem level. I'll bet Donna keeps all her recipe information at the subsystem, or sub-menu level in her case, right? Just makes sense. It gives her many more accessible options for creating a complete meal."

Dennis, who'd been attentive but quiet, said, "Wait a minute. That's not fair. Surely, all those 243 combinations wouldn't be compatible."

"They could be," Jan responded quickly. "Provided all the assembly points were standardized, you could theoretically build 243 working and distinct bikes. Realistically, of course, you probably wouldn't be able to because of different wheel sizes and corresponding frames, but I think you get the point. All the subsystems should have comparative data, the tradeoff curves, that would allow bicycles to be built to varying targets of performance and features."

I nodded my agreement. I could tell that everyone was buying into the logic.

"Now I want to talk about 'innovation to risk' ratio," Jan said as she put up her next slide (Figure 5e).

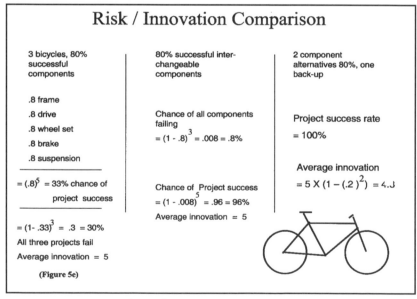

Risk / Innovation Comparison

3 bicycles, 80% successful components

.8 frame
.8 drive
.8 wheel set
.8 brake
.8 suspension

$= (.8)^5$ = 33% chance of project success

$= (1 - .33)^3 = .3 = 30\%$
All three projects fail
Average innovation = 5

(Figure 5e)

80% successful inter-changeable components

Chance of all components failing
$= (1 - .8)^3 = .008 = .8\%$

Chance of Project success
$= (1 - .008)^5 = .96 = 96\%$
Average innovation = 5

2 component alternatives 80%, one back-up

Project success rate
= 100%

Average innovation
$= 5 \times (1 - (.2)^2) = 4.3$

"You'd expect that the more innovation you design into a project, the more risk you'd have. Therefore, there's always a tradeoff that must be made on any project. The set-based approach allows more innovation with less risk, which gives a distinct competitive advantage. Assume you design three bicycles with the point-based process, each with eighty percent successfully designed components. There's only a thirty-three percent chance of success for any project, and a thirty percent chance all three projects will fail, right?"

Several minutes of discussion followed, everyone trying to remember their statistics. Luckily, Greg, our Six Sigma blackbelt, was able to lead us.

Jan continued, "Let's assume we design the three bicycles with interchangeable sets of components, each with the same eighty percent success rate. The chance that any component will totally fail is only point eight percent and the chance for project success is ninety-six percent. If you use redundancy with one proven backup for each component, the risk goes to zero, with still a significant amount of innovation."

As might be expected with a bunch of engineers, a lot of discussion ensued on the math. But we all agreed the basics were correct and significant.

Lori said, "Gosh, I wasn't expecting a math class today, but I think I get it. No wonder we have long loopbacks. They're inevitable in a point-based system."

Jan nodded. "Absolutely, think about what happens in our military business. In our initial proposal to the DoD, we define a rather complete view of the system concept that will theoretically meet the contract requirements. Then we design subsystem specs accordingly. As the subsystem designs fail, a cycle of spec and design changes ripples through all subsystems. You might call our design process, 'fail and react.' Our best managers are the best firefighters. How many times do we ignore some new great possibility because we know its ramifications could not be absorbed by the project? And even worse, that new idea might well be lost forever since we have no defined means for capturing it." She shrugged. "Just think of the power if the entire project was built around exploring all of these possibilities, rather than reacting to the failure of only a few."

"Let's talk about cost." She put up her next slide (Figure 5f).

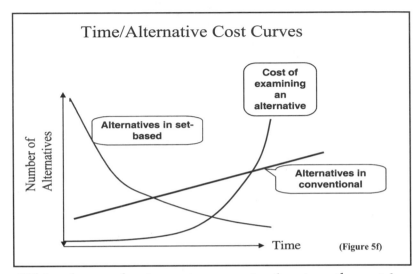

Time/Alternative Cost Curves

(Figure 5f)

"This shows the impact on cost of using the set-based approach. Conventionally, the cost of examining an alternative significantly increases over the life of the project because of the broad impact of changes in the later stages of design. In set-based, the alternatives are explored early in the process when costs are less. The result is more innovation in less time and much less cost."

She quickly put up her next slide (Figure 5g), which showed typical overall results on total project costs.

"The solid-line curve is what we always want our cost curve to look like. The resources ramp up quickly, level out, and then drop rapidly during final testing and hand-off into production. Unfortunately, the curve almost always looks like the dash line. The resources peak later because engineers are bogged down on other programs, but they also peak higher and extend longer because of firefighting, confusion, and delays in decision-making."

Dick said, "Yep, absolutely, and we always try to figure out why. According to your logic, the result is preordained. I'd like to argue with you, but I have to admit, that seems to be the case. Does anyone remember that project when Grant tried to force the curve on the left by staffing the people early?"

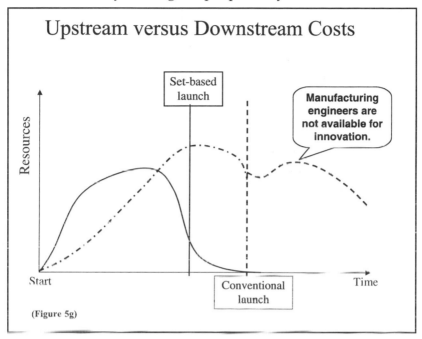

(Figure 5g)

Laughing, Vijay said, "It was amazing. He took resources from several projects already in trouble to preload that one."

I asked, "So what happened?"

Dick shook his head. "The project ended up looking like the one on the right, but the curve was about twice as high. He fired the program manager about a year later."

After a lull in the discussion, Jan said, "That's as far as I was going to go on set-based concurrent engineering. What do you think?"

Tim said, "Jan, I've got to admit the numbers are compelling. I'm still not convinced we can make it work, but I'm not as negative as I was yesterday. I'll stick around for the rest of your story." He paused for a moment, then added, "It does seem that this set-based theory is the core concept of the Toyota product development system. Is this correct?"

"I think that is a fair statement." Jan responded. "Okay, tell me what can be done to make it work?"

Greg said, "I'll bite. In all likelihood, it's not going to work unless the workforce has the technical expertise and the discipline to execute the set-based process—and unless there's technical leadership that's willing and capable of making accurate and timely decisions, and also unless there's some sort of scheduling and planning system to allow the flexibility for innovation."

Carl jumped in. "Greg, you cheated. That was all on Jan's four corner chart from earlier. But it does make sense. I think all those things you mentioned are all absolutely necessary. But is that really all that's required?"

"Good question," Jan responded. "I think the answer is a qualified yes. But the transition from an administrative system like ours might be tough since we'd have to fix a lot of things. Let me walk through the other fundamentals. First, let's talk about the workforce. It's their knowledge that has to make it work. Let me talk about how Toyota does it." She went to the board and wrote:

The engineer is responsible and rewarded for performance.

"Our reward system is based on rapid promotion of the engineer into management. Most engineers do not get more than one design cycle, if that. Would anyone here go to a surgeon that had performed only one successful surgery?" She shrugged. "Of course not. Nobody in our management actually knows who the good engineers are. If you know the process lingo, if you know the right people, and if you present well, you can get good raises. At Toyota, you're clearly responsible for your part of the design and are rewarded for performance in terms of what you do for the customer, and your ability to add knowledge. The more design cycles you get, the more knowledgeable you are and the more you get paid. So engineers continue to do engineering. Pretty simple concept, actually."

She added to the board:

Tradeoff curves are the central core of knowledge.

"At Toyota, the engineers systematically keep and communicate their knowledge through tradeoff curves and analysis results based on their subsystem testing. In my opinion, if we were using set-based and had dedicated engineers, there's no reason we wouldn't end up with similar curves. In other words, the tradeoff curves become the language of set-based design. Having multiple possibilities does no good unless there's a corresponding way to capture and use comparative knowledge across projects. In my opinion, for IRT, we'd define standard formats for our version of tradeoff curves, which would be integrated into our corporate information systems."

Tim said, "Jan, I agree in principle, but how do you get started? That's what concerns me."

Jan said, "I agree. That's an issue for transition." She went back to the board and added:

Functional managers are teachers.

"At Toyota, the functional managers are primarily teachers. In fact, they'd have to be for the system to work. The engineers are expected to be individually responsible. They have to learn from their managers. Managers at Toyota are the most technically competent engineers with the most experience. Does this make sense?"

I was reminded of what Donna had said about her grandmother and mother-in-law being her mentors while she was learning to cook.

Jan continued. "The functional managers are also responsible for the completeness and control of the tradeoff curves. In fact, these tradeoff curves and analysis data are the standards that they live by, the same way we do with respect to our quality procedures and process documentation. That's all I was going to cover regarding the workforce."

She took a breath. "Now let's talk about the project leadership needed to make the set-based process work. Based on what we've talked about so far, who can give me some requirements?"

Tim responded, "Well, it sounds like if the functional managers are responsible for the teaching and the technical excellence of the individual designs, then the project leadership must be responsible for managing the set-based process and somehow converging on a solution from lots of possibilities and no specs. That seems like a tough job."

"That's good," Jan replied. "In fact, at Toyota, it is the project leader's—or chief engineer's—car, totally. He deals with the customer, finds the resources, and makes the combining and narrowing decisions. The people don't report to him, except for a small integrating staff. He will negotiate with the functional managers for people and for design quality. Pretty straightforward really."

"The chief engineers are recognized as the best engineers in the company and are revered. They each have at least twenty years of design experience in more than one area of expertise. They have strong personalities, and in their relationships with the functional managers, are expected to be confrontational in obtaining resources and demanding technical excellence. Their reward for being a good chief engineer is the privilege of doing it again."

Dick asked Tim and Vijay whether they thought we had enough leaders with the proper skills to take on that role today in a set-based environment. This discussion took awhile, but in the end it was agreed that we did. But it would mean that a lot of the system engineering organization might have to take on that role.

An interesting side discussion took place on the potential role of the many excellent engineers on our technical promotion ladder. IRT had created this track to recognize engineers that didn't have the desire or the skills for the normal progression into administrative management. The question that lingered was, would they become the new organizational leaders?

Carl asked Jan, "Do you think this has to be done exactly like Toyota—particularly in the transition?"

"No, I don't," Jan said. "I think it could be a two-person team performing that role. Denso actually does that. The important thing is that whatever we set up would have to make the set-based process possible. Let's move to the last cornerstone, how we schedule and control the project."

Jan waited for concurrence. She'd done a good job so far of making this entire thing seem possible. I was curious to see how time was managed in this emergence process.

Jan said, "What's true about our scheduling and control process?"

Jay answered, "It seldom, if ever, works as planned. Delays accumulate. We lose confidence in the plan. Manual 'hot' scheduling takes over."

"True enough, but why?" Jan asked.

Carl said, "Several reasons. The way we plan is task-based. One task completion triggers other tasks to start. Even our current process is not based on static tasks but on the largely unpredictable results that then drive the subsequent activities. Our entire approach is just not flexible enough to account for the natural variability of product development. It's a push system that gives our administrative management an illusion of control through our design reviews. And as you know, these view task completions as progress."

I said, "That about covers it. I don't think Carl is a fan of our system."

Jan answered, "Whew, I guess not, but let me emphasize the key point. It's the nature of product development that there will be variability. There has to be if there's going to be innovation. In addition, tasks to be done in the future will be defined based on

135

the results of current tasks. Laying out the tasks for an entire product development project at the beginning of the project has got to be the height of planning arrogance. So why do we try? Because we have a schedule to keep and we don't know any other way to do it—and our administrative management loves the structure." She shook her head. "So let's talk about what it takes to support the set-based process. The Toyota system is 'responsibility-based' as opposed to 'task-based.' The chief engineer sets a number of target times for key integrating events, such as styling approval or a major tooling release. This is when things have to come together, so he establishes exactly what needs to be ready at those times. Everyone understands—these dates are *never* missed. Some subsystem alternatives might miss the window, but there's always a backup standing by. He then sets responsibilities for the results. It's the responsibility of those involved to work out their schedules to meet the dates, and to communicate the plan to those who need to know. Now remember, we have a responsible workforce involved here. The chief engineer and his staff will consolidate the plans as needed to ensure confidence and coordination. Also, understand that design reviews are different in this environment. They're hands on, with highly technical managers reviewing the results of a highly knowledgeable workforce. It's also here that the combining and narrowing set-based decisions are made. The results are looked at for technical merit and decision making, rather than to see how many tasks have been completed. Toyota does heavy prototyping to support these reviews, as well as to create real knowledge for the tradeoff curves and decisions."

Jay asked sarcastically, "You mean they don't care how many trivial drawings are completed?"

Dick said, "Do you remember the EYEHAWK program that I discussed a couple of days ago? It was without a doubt the best program I ever managed. We started out traditionally. We tailored the PDSP process that created our schedule chart, and we began our traditional process. We had two mechanical engineers and a system engineer that had different ideas. They had become very proficient in Pro/E, our CAD system. They decided to not make drawings until the end of the project. They worked with manufacturing and our casting suppliers using only databases. This allowed a really great concurrent engineering environment. We completed the project on schedule, under budget, and with the highest quality ever released into manufacturing. Yet we were continually abused during design reviews because our scheduling system always showed us behind. It was actually humorous trying to explain to some of our managers that we were ahead of schedule when, three-fourths of the way through the project, we had no drawings completed. In reality, the success of the project has never been recognized. I lost all three of those engineers—and it wasn't exactly career enhancing for me. Sorry for venting."

I said, "Maybe not *yet* career enhancing."

"Yeah, maybe," Dick added. "But it was the most fun I've ever had at IRT. We operated on the cornerstones of the knowledge-based system. We didn't really do set-based concurrent engineering, but I'll bet we could have."

Jan put up a new slide illustrating the differences (Figure 5h).

"This chart summarizes the differences between our current system and the knowledge-based approach. In both cases you'll have a schedule, but in the responsibility-based approach, you'll have accountability, ownership, and rapid response flexibility. The schedules might look similar but the differences are night and day. Notice that in the task-based system, the planning and execution are done by different people, often even by different organizations. They almost always degrade over time, and there's significant waste as everyone tries to keep the damn things current to what's really happening. On the other hand, the responsibility-based approach keeps execution aligned, since the overall schedule is simply the compilation of all the personal plans."

Tim said, "I'm struggling to see the difference. I agree our

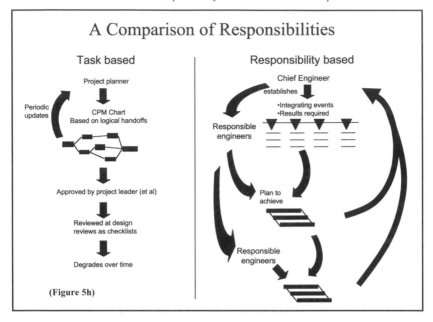

A Comparison of Responsibilities

Task based

Project planner

Periodic updates

CPM Chart
Based on logical handoffs

Approved by project leader (et al)

Reviewed at design
reviews as checklists

Degrades over time

(Figure 5h)

Responsibility based

Chief Engineer
establishes

•Integrating events
•Results required

Responsible
engineers

Plan to
achieve

Responsible
engineers

current planning system seldom holds together until the end of the project, but what makes the Toyota system work so much better?"

"Several things," Jan said. "First, the integrating events are imperative dates, which means they will not slip. Logical integrating events for IRT would be 'detector selection,' 'optics path approval,' and probably 'housing casting release'. These are all dates that drive both product delivery and the narrowing of design choices. That knowledge forces the engineers to always have suitable backups, since they're responsible, as we discussed earlier. There are also highly technical managers who're ensuring it all comes together. Status reviews are never based on tasks completed, but on technical results. In reality, the engineering staff is completely focused on meeting the targets at integrating events. The dates of the events have a lot more meaning than our task-based milestones. I've seen us shortchange tasks, like drawing count, to meet our milestones. Realistically, it seems that so many of our design reviews are just exercises in wishful thinking. Toyota simply has a different mindset. The integrating events are for decision making and to ensure the overall schedule is met. Again, they are never missed."

After pausing and taking a breath, Jan continued. "A really good analogy and probably the benchmark for responsibility-based planning and control is modern U.S. military war planning. Top-down detailed planning and execution have been replaced by top-down objectives, but with the detailed planning and execution by the field commanders based on what is actually happening. This allows multiple possibilities to be explored while staying within the context of well-defined, overall objectives. In fact, this planning approach has been put to use with very good results by the U.S. military in recent conflicts. To me, it was humorous to watch TV pundits criticizing the military plans, when in reality, they didn't understand the planning philosophy."

"I can buy into the differences, and I like your analogy," Tim said. "Also, I reluctantly agree with your assessment that our design reviews are too often technically shallow. As a Toyota manager, I'd put all of my skills into understanding the technical compliance and tradeoffs at the integrating events as opposed to counting task completions. I'd also focus primarily on looking over the engineer's shoulders as opposed to relying on formal reviews for my technical understanding. It seems to me that the reason the Toyota managers are so technical is that they have to be if they are going to make it all work."

Jan said, "Sounds right to me." She seemed pleased Tim was more positive today. "In fact, the Toyota managers are famous for continually asking 'why' when they make their engineering rounds until they get to the bottom-line answer. We've all seen the concept on TV medical shows as the lead doctor makes rounds with student doctors and asks a lot of questions. Same thing."

Tim continued, "Jan, yesterday I had trouble believing that Toyota's product development solutions just emerge—as you put it. In reality, they have redundant solution sets against flexible targets, hard integrating events, personal planning by competent

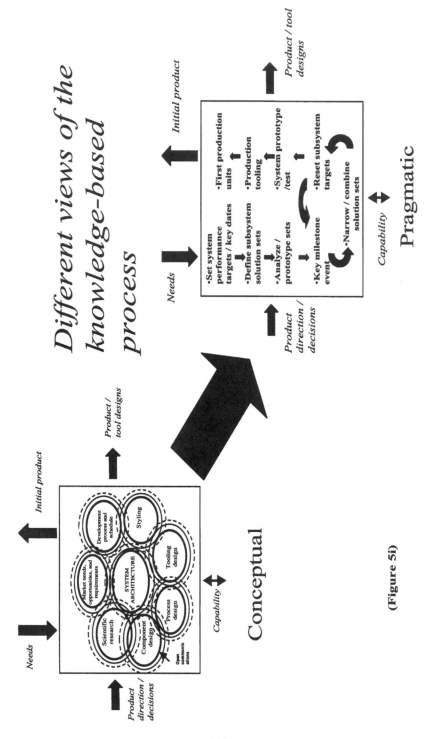

Different views of the knowledge-based process

Conceptual

Pragmatic

Needs

Initial product

Product / tool designs

Product direction / decisions

Capability

Needs

Initial product

Product / tool designs

Product direction / decisions

Capability

- Set system performance targets / key dates
- Define subsystem solution sets
- Analyze / prototype sets
- Key milestone event
- First production units
- Production tooling
- System prototype /test
- Reset subsystem targets
- Narrow / combine solution sets

Development process and schedule

Styling

Tooling design

Process design

Component design

Scientific research

Market needs, opportunities, and requirements

SYSTEM ARCHITECTURE

Open communications

(Figure 5i)

140

engineers, and technical managers who can pull it all together. I can accept that this seems like a better system than ours." He paused. "I think we have the technical talent. But it wouldn't be easy to completely change the way we work."

Jan gave me a pleading look. "Jon, can we take a break? I'm worn out."

"Sure," I said. "You've done a nice job explaining this." Everyone seemed in much better spirits today. Jan had made the knowledge-based environment seem more real. "In fact, why don't we break for a long lunch? Sorry we took so long without a break. Let's be back at one."

Greg and I had lunch together. We agreed the focus of the meeting with Jack should be on the potential results that could be achieved by using the knowledge-based approach. This would be an attack on every sacred cow in our processes. We didn't know what would happen, but Jack had told us to be bold. He wouldn't be disappointed in that regard. Unfortunately, we didn't have a plan that would show how to make the change. That was our Achilles' heel. We needed some ideas to come out of this afternoon's discussion.

We returned to the room at one o'clock. Before I could say anything, Tim asked if he could have a few minutes. He said he'd thought more about actually making the system work from his perspective as a program manager. "Yesterday, Dick and I had problems with that circular emergence chart. It was too theoretical for us. We feel a little better after this morning's discussion. See if this makes sense—We put it together over lunch. Hope you don't mind, Jon. We got the PowerPoint masters from your secretary." He shook his head. "Tell you what. She's something else." Tim put up a new slide that showed a different way of looking at the knowledge-based process (Figure 5i).

Tim continued, "All we did was replace the conceptual emergence chart with one that defines a logical series of target or integrating events. We like the chart on the left from a conceptual perspective, but the one on the right seems more doable. Over time, Dick and I believe we can define real events, potentially with our customer, that double as integrating events and key milestones for progress."

Jan said, "That is exactly what Toyota does. Major events like styling approval force narrowing decisions, and at the same time are key project milestones."

Dick added, "If so, our entire process standardization might be to select these key milestones for each of our businesses, as opposed to using the detailed process we have today. Then we would have a more pragmatic view of the process built around the key imperative events within a cyclic process of combining, narrowing and resetting subsystems targets."

I really liked what Tim had done. It was easy to see a knowledge-based approach working only in a company made up of super-smart engineers, as we suspected was the case with Toyota. Therefore, we needed heavy-duty structure to control our engineers. The truth was, having a few key events as milestones and allowing our engineers to manage themselves was probably the way to be successful.

Tim took his slide off and sat down, and Vijay walked to the front of the room.

"Well," he said, "Jan and I were also busy at lunch. A couple of days ago in our analysis, we judged all of our initiatives as largely ineffective for resolving our key issues (Figures 3j). Jan and I took a shot at the same thing, but using each of the four cornerstones of the knowledge-based, or lean environment." He then put up the revised chart (Figure 5j).

"In our opinion, at least one of the lean cornerstones resolves each of our key issues."

I was amazed. Their chart made so much sense, it required very little discussion. It also brought home that success would take simultaneous implementation of all the cornerstones. We agreed that not resolving any of these key issues would be a major

Current Initiative Effectiveness

	Set-based Process	Engineering leadership	Responsibility Based planning	Workforce Expertise
Administrative Leadership	I	R	I	0
Low value-added effort	I	I	R	I
Ineffective design reviews	R	R	R	I
Pseudo concurrent engineering	R	0	I	I
Minimal learning between projects	R	0	0	I
Low engineering experience	I	I	I	R
Inaccurate scheduling	0	I	R	I
Long design loop backs	R	I	I	0

R = resolves   I = Improves   0 = no change   -- = makes worse

(Figure 5j)

problem, which indicated a strong need for change.

I stood up. "Let me summarize. It seems as though we all agree that the knowledge-based environment can meet our goals, even though we haven't done an exact analysis. I think we all agree at this point that we don't see an alternative. And I think we all realize how difficult the change is going to be."

Carl added, "It may be impossible. We've never been successful at implementing major initiatives around this company. We just replace one with another and move on."

"I agree," I said. "We need to talk about that."

Greg stood up. "Before we do, I have another problem that we need to discuss. Six Sigma. This is a major effort at IRT and all across the country. I realize that Toyota doesn't appear to have this kind of dedicated program for Six Sigma. I understand also that they might just have the best quality in the business. Is everybody else wrong? I think we need to understand this."

He was right. So much had been written about Six Sigma being the savior. Zealots were everywhere devoted to the cause. We did need to address it in context with the knowledge-based environment. I said, "Good point—let's think it through. Greg, give me a definition of Six Sigma."

Greg said, "I knew you were going to ask that, so I've pulled several slides out of my files. Actually, there are a number of different definitions. I'll quote you one from the book, *The Six Sigma Way* by Pande, Neuman, and Cavanagh." He opened the book, and read, "Six Sigma can be defined in several ways. It's a way of measuring processes; a goal of near-perfection, represented by 3.4 defects per million opportunities (DPMO); an approach to changing the culture of the organization. Most accurately, though, Six Sigma is defined as a broad and comprehensive system for building and sustaining business performance, success, and leadership. In other words, Six Sigma is a context within which you will be able to integrate many valuable but often disconnected management 'best practices' and concepts, including systems thinking, continuous improvement, knowledge management, mass customization, and activity-based management." Greg then shifted to some notes. "Here are a couple of other excerpts from other definitions: 'a structured application of the tools and techniques of TQM,' a 'philosophy of doing business with a focus on eliminating defects through fundamental process knowledge.' All the approaches use a systematic process of define-measure-analyze-improve-control."

I said, "Greg, it appears to me that based on these definitions, Six Sigma, the basis of which is the effective ability to measure quality, is *primarily* an approach for companies to measure and continuously improve the results of their structured processes. That would explain why it makes good sense with regard to manufacturing, which is structural by nature." I shrugged. "On the other hand, it'd seem to be more difficult to apply in product development except as a predictive measure for the product that's under development. It's also understandable why a knowledge-based company like Toyota wouldn't use a structured approach like Six Sigma. Yet I could argue, as you mentioned earlier, that Toyota certainly has the best quality in its market. It would appear that their design process of solution sets, redundant designs, and technical focus will naturally and consistently produce high quality products."

Jan added, "I agree with your comments. Our NCMS project also struggled with this issue. We concluded that 'Design for Six Sigma (DFSS)' made more sense from the product development perspective. That since Six Sigma really is a measure intended for the product as the customer sees it, the ability to predict the results while still in the development stage is very important. That would tell me that DFSS should be a definite part of a knowledge-based product development environment."

Greg pulled out another paper. "In fact, let me quote a definition of DFSS from Dr. Phil Samuel, from a recent conference I attended. Design for Six Sigma is the deliberate act of designing a product, process, or service, resulting in an entity that exhibits Six Sigma levels of performance in all dimensions of risk."

Vijay said, "Doesn't that describe the Toyota process?"

After a few minutes of discussion, we concluded that Toyota inherently had a strong design for Six Sigma strategy. In effect, their process naturally delivered high quality with the result that they've never needed to focus on it. We were curious to know if they actually made DPMO calculations. Regardless, we all decided that any knowledge-based development environment should include predictive measurements of DPMO as one of the targets and narrowing criteria. Over time this would lead to a series of tradeoff curves based upon DFSS principles. This made perfect sense to me. We were using Six Sigma knowledge but not focusing on all the structure that had been built on top of it.

Greg commented, "Okay, I feel better. We can move on."

I decided to turn to the change problem. "The last subject that I wanted to cover today was how to make the change happen. Any thoughts?"

Greg laughed. "I have no clue, and we can't possibly figure that out in the next hour." Carl seemed to be pretty worn out, as did everyone. "Why don't you ask your secretary? She always seems to be a step ahead of us."

I said, "Actually, she did have an answer. She just said that over time, as the engineers gained the knowledge, the problem would take care of itself. You know, she may actually have a point."

Tim said, "Maybe, but Jack wants the change in a year, and we have to put the basics in place for all the four cornerstones—the set-based process, the flow scheduling system, the workforce expertise, and a new leadership focus for both the people and the projects. Most important, everybody is going to have to look at everything so differently. Jon, I'd suggest we only focus on selling the knowledge-based philosophy for Monday. We have to assume we can make the change. As opposed to yesterday, I feel we can, although it won't be easy."

I agreed. Everybody was relieved I wasn't going to have them work on Saturday to put the pitch together. Amazingly, the team seemed to have bought into the knowledge-based principles as the basis for our projected product development environment, although nobody, including myself, had much confidence in our ability to change. It would be difficult, however, to go to Jack on Monday and propose such a strategic change with only logic and the word from a rather junior consortium team.

I arrived back at my office at about four o'clock. Donna had left a note on my desk to call Allen Ward. I dialed his number, wondering whether to call him Dr. Ward or Allen.

"Hello. This is Al Ward,"

"Hi, Al, this is Jon Stevens from IRT Corporation. Thanks for returning my call. Have you got a few minutes?"

"Sure," he said. "All the time you need."

I spent the next few minutes going over our dilemma and the

146

activities of our team including a summary of Jan's comments. I concluded my introduction by imploring him to give me something, anything to bolster my confidence.

Al remembered Jan from the NCMS project and was complementary of her grasp of knowledge-based fundamentals. After listening and asking a few questions, Al said, "Jon, I know that you are hoping I can give you many more case studies that prove the knowledge-based environment is the silver bullet that you're looking for, but I can't. However, there are some companies that are starting to see some significant progress. One is Thermo CRS Limited, a business unit of Thermo Electron Corporation. They build automation products for the pharmaceutical and biotechnology industries. I recently talked to Dr. Roger Hertz, who's Vice President over R&D. He's seen some encouraging results after phasing in many of the concepts over the last eighteen months. He's reported an increase in patent applications of 500%, 93% on-time milestone completions versus zero percent previously, and extremely smooth manufacturing startups. They're also estimating a 2.7 times gain in value-added productivity, which is really significant. These improvements, I believe, are characteristic of companies making the transition.

"Also, we've had successes on programs at Delphi. In fact, the Delphi-Rochester plant claimed a three-times throughput gain, and dramatically reduced the design-build-test cycle-time to just one day on some products. But other than Toyota and Denso, there are no companies I know of that have deployed this philosophy company-wide. Nevertheless, we're seeing strong glimpses into the potential with the pioneering efforts at Thermo CRS and Delphi.

"However," he continued, "this isn't a situation where you're talking about spending a bunch of money on a new tool and you need justification that it'll pay back. Let me give you an analogy. Overweight people will spend a lot of money on weight-loss products on the basis of marketing hype and supposed case studies. They justify the cost of the product based on their perceived potential weight loss. On the other hand, some people correctly understand that successful weight loss is about a change in life style, not the tools of weight-loss. Does this make sense?"

I laughed. "Jan said to look out for you since you come from the world of academia, but what I think you're saying is if someone is going to use weight-loss products, or the tools of weight loss, they need case studies and proof that the tools work. If on the other hand, they're going to change to a logical, healthier lifestyle with more exercise and healthier foods, then hard justification isn't needed. Pure logic is enough. The analogy obviously is that the knowledge-based environment is a healthier lifestyle in the product development world."

"You get an A in comprehension," Al said in the voice of a college professor. "Now, let me try to prove the logic to you. Write this on a sheet of paper, then we'll talk about it." Over the next few minutes, he dictated what he described as a characterization of the product development environment (Figure 5k).

Al said, "The column in the middle shows the key elements of the product development environment. They are the **process** that is the actual work that's done to create the product, the **leadership** that's the decision-making within the project, the **planning and control** of the project which is obviously setting and managing the schedule, and the **engineering workforce** that actually does the work. These would be analogous to exercise, healthy eating, stress management, and so on in our healthy lifestyle analogy. I think we can agree that these elements are important keys to successful product development."

I agreed, and he continued, "Now let's look at each element and the two extremes as to the fundamental paradigms that companies use. We believe the paradigms will pull the right tools, but not the reverse. Companies continually put in new tools, or initiatives, but unless they somehow change how they think about the problem, nothing lasting will ever really happen." He again al

Product Development Environments

Traditional PD	Key PD Elements	Knowledge-based (Toyota)
One/two concepts / One perspective	—— Process ——	Many alternatives / many perspectives
Administrative	—— Leadership ——	Technical / coaching
Based on inflexible tasks	—— Planning / control ——	Based on flexible results
Diverse responsibilities	—— Workforce ——	Individual excellence / personal responsibility

(Figure 5k)

waited for my acknowledgement, then continued, "The traditionprocess paradigm is based on picking a few system concepts from generally one perspective. The other extreme is continually evaluating many alternatives from many different perspectives. Intuitively, the right extreme seems superior, provided of course it can be accomplished—which Toyota and Denso have proven it can."

I said, "What do you mean by different perspectives?"

He said, "Typically, companies seem to approach the solution from one viewpoint, such as software scheme, system packaging, or electronics design. Toyota looks at all perspectives—manufacturing, packaging, support, software, whatever—as key potential drivers of the final design. If it can be done, this has got to be a better paradigm."

I said, "Thank you. I understand and agree."

"On Leadership," he said, "one extreme is the traditional administrative project management that's characterized by the counting of tasks as the primary focus of project reviews. The design content is left to other teams or whatever the project uses for decision making. Often, in my experience, hard decisions are never really made, but are backed into as the project fights its way through problems and runs short of money and time. The other extreme is a leadership environment where the project managers understand the technical issues, make timely decisions, and lead through coaching. It's a fundamentally better way."

He paused for a moment, then continued. "The traditional view of planning and control is to establish a sequence of tasks, assign people to the tasks, and keep track of the completion status of the tasks. In reality, in product development, the ability to define all the tasks in sequence is next to impossible. Therefore, the entire project is one of working around the defined schedules and plans. The truth is, future product development tasks are driven primarily by the results of the prior tasks, and therefore can't be predetermined. A better paradigm is to distribute the planning and control to those who understand and can react to the interim results, and of course that would be the responsible engineers. Modern warfare is a good example. In the past, wars were conducted from the rear through maps and models. Today, field commanders are responsible for tactical decisions in reaction to what's really happening. This was a fundamental paradigm shift, similar in many ways to our product development situation. And finally, the traditional workforce has become a collection of engineers, teams, and functional personnel that may or may not be fully qualified to execute the tasks. This is *seemingly* okay in a task-based environment, because how well the tasks are done is often minimized in a world that counts the number of tasks completed as the basic measure of progress. In a results-based environment, deficient engineering stands out like a sore thumb and isn't tolerated.

"Jon," he concluded, "I believe that any movement of a company's product development process toward the right side of the chart is positive and will pull the behaviors and tools to make it successful. I'm aware that you can view this explanation as a cop-out from any real justification of the knowledge-based environment, and I wish I had a real transformation of a company I could show you. Personally, I've been frustrated by not being in a position to do that. We've certainly seen isolated successes, but until now have had no real commitment to transform an entire product development environment at any company. But, as I've said, I've no doubt that any movement toward the right side of the chart will yield positive results. I don't perceive any risk in making these changes. At the bare minimum, you'll expose some engineering issues that should be corrected. If you succeed, you'll be world class. Either way, you'll have gotten people involved and will be a better company."

I replied, "Those are good points, Allen. Our team's been worried about the difficulty of making the change, but realistically, any progress toward the knowledge-based environment would be positive. How can you go wrong with more focus on coaching and personal involvement—regardless of how far you get?"

After a few more minutes of discussion, I decided I'd absorbed all I could at one time. Al was certainly willing to help and seemed excited about what appeared to be a mandate from Jack for real change. The one-year time frame concerned him. He didn't know if that was possible. We agreed to talk after my presentation.

As I drove home, I thought about what I'd heard. Al really hadn't given me much more information than I'd gotten from Jan—just verification and another viewpoint. It was clear, however, that IRT was on the far left of Al's chart and had all the problems he had discussed. It was also clear that Jack wanted real change. From a strictly logical perspective, the idea of establishing a paradigm shift in product development seemed sound, based on the high level of quality and productivity enjoyed by Toyota.

DISCUSSION

From a change perspective, this part of the process, transforming the vision into reality, is the transition between a vision in theory and implementation. It is also where the analysis and evaluation of options occurs. There could be multiple possibilities considered at this step, but only one system should emerge at the conclusion.

Illustrated in the story are several factors that must be considered during this transition.

1. The vision must be put in operational terms.

In the case of knowledge-based development, the project leadership, the planning and control of programs, the responsibilities of the workforce, and the development process specifics were all addressed so that the evaluator could understand the potential impact on each. Details must be scrutinized in order for confidence to be built that the change can be made without undue difficulty. In fact, the new paradigm will likely begin to lose its identity to some degree after it is broken into components. In other words, the vision will become the sum of its operational parts. If a vision cannot be effectively broken into basic elements, I believe the vision is too abstract to be realized and needs to be rethought. The vision has to be perceived as a workable system.

2. The vision (system) must resolve the fundamental issues.

The new paradigm in its operational form must resolve the fundamental issues that initiated the search. Ideally, this would be based on quantitative analysis, but qualitative judgment may have to suffice. Unfortunately, administrative management at most manufacturing companies prefers hard payback calculations, which can be difficult to come by for comprehensive visionary changes. Engineering intuition and risk analysis must play important roles in large-scale changes.

3. *Don't leave loose ends.*

All areas of concern, sacred cows, workforce capabilities, and so forth, must be brought into the open and discussed. Loose ends seem invariably to get caught in the "wishful thinking syndrome." Eventually, these will have to be dealt with or they can easily deep-six a well-intentioned change process. In the case of IRT, the strong Six Sigma initiative and its relationship with knowledge-based development had to be identified and resolved early. The embedded-quality approach found in knowledge-based development is incompatible with a Six Sigma testing strategy that attempts to drive quality into products. Embedding Six Sigma analysis concepts within set-based exploration, however, does make perfect sense.

When I was with Texas Instruments, we had a strong initiative to define detailed functional processes. We also had a strong business process reengineering initiative. The owners of each had not resolved some basic definition issues. As a result, the inconsistencies between the concepts of functional processes and business processes were a constant source of confusion.

Loose ends will always become problems, or as Murphy's Law states, "Anything that can go wrong, will."

The next change step is to gain commitment to the new paradigm.

Chapter 6

Committing to the Future
(The Power of Visionary Leadership)

Top-level leadership must continually communicate commitment. The first task is to create a sense of urgency through the case for action. The second is to establish a vision of the future state, along with clear goals. Without the leader's unwavering commitment, keeping the change process focused and on track is all but impossible.

Saturday morning, Jon's home

It was about eight in the morning when Troy called. "Our tee time is ten-thirty. Are you going to play?"

"I'm tempted," I said. "But the meeting with Jack is at nine o'clock on Monday. I think I'd better put my pitch together."

"Yeah, I figured that would be your answer, but I thought I'd ask." Then he said, "So, what breakthroughs did you come up with?"

"Well," I said, "we found a company that's four times more productive than we are, operating with a totally different philosophy concerning process, leadership, responsibility, and project management. I'm going to recommend we follow their lead."

First there was dead air. Then Troy gave me some honest advice, which I appreciated. Although his volatility had often gotten him in trouble, he had the unique capability of quickly getting to the bottom line. "I think you're doing the right thing by being bold. Knowing Jack, I think he really wants someone, namely

154

you, to have the guts to propose something totally different to shake things up. It would be inappropriate for him to just come in and start whopping people in the head. He wants to react off of you. Also, don't go into too much detail. Jorgenson and Osgood will be looking for openings to discredit you. And my last advice: don't propose that we look just like that other company—Toyota, right? If you do, we'll always be playing catch-up. I think we have a great bunch of people at this company. You should use them to define our culture around the Toyota principles." I heard him exhale. "There, I feel much better. You haven't asked me for a damn thing all week, but I decided to throw in my two cents worth, anyway."

"Thanks, Troy, good advice," I answered sincerely. "But how did you know we were looking at Toyota?"

He responded matter-of-factly. "Donna and I go pretty far back and she's also a little miffed that I wasn't on your team. Gotta go. Gonna have breakfast at the club. Love their biscuits."

As soon as I hung up, the phone rang again. It was Jack. "Good morning, Jon. Hope I didn't wake you or Penny." After a few more pleasantries, he got to the point of his call, which was to get himself comfortable with the meeting. "Are you ready for Monday?"

I said, "Not yet. I'll be putting my slides together today. Did you want to see them before the meeting?"

"No, no, absolutely not," he said. "I want to see them when everyone else does. You're going to make a case for major change, right?"

"Oh, yes," I said, thinking that that was an understatement. "So how were your meetings?" I asked, looking for any insight that might help my presentation.

"This week I talked to our customers in the DoD, automotive, and security industries. I also talked to our people in marketing and research. We have an incredible opportunity. Everyone seems to see the benefits of what infrared technology can do, and we have the best low-cost technology as far as I can tell. And it's locked up for the next couple of years. If we can develop a flow of products quickly into those markets, we can dominate them all. Our old high-end marketplace is dead, even for the military, and we only have a little time. By the way, did Jan show up? I enjoyed talking to her. Her husband was a little difficult."

"Oh, yes. She showed up all right. Her material is the basis for our recommendation."

"Good. Gotta go. Tell Penny hello. I'll see you Monday."

After he hung up, I realized that Troy was right on the mark. Jack didn't really expect much from me except to shake things up. That realization made the presentation a little easier, but I must admit the thought was a little damaging to my ego. As I opened up PowerPoint, I decided that it was knowledge-based or bust.

Monday morning, IRT Corporation.

On the drive in, as was usual before a major presentation, I spent the time going over slides in my head. I'd learned that I wasn't prepared if I had to look at them. Everything just had to flow together. I felt ready, but this pitch was unlike so much of what I'd done in the past, most of which was resolving technical problems. So I kept reminding myself that Jack wasn't really expecting that much.

Donna was there when I walked in. "Give me your floppy, I'll clean it up and make the slides. How many copies?"

"None," I said as I handed her my diskette. I thought I'd found any misspelled words, but somehow, I was always inconsistent on fonts. Donna was great on making these things look professional. She hated the fact that now we all prepared our own presentations.

I gave her my diskette and headed to the cafeteria, wishing the meeting were at eight. I hated to wait around.

After I got coffee, I saw Troy in his usual spot, reading the paper. "So. Are you ready?"

I sat down. "You never know on these things. I took your advice. Kept it simple."

"Good," he said. "Let's have lunch and you can debrief me. Now, let's talk golf."

He talked me into playing golf in the afternoon with the argument that I deserved a break after the meeting.

Back at my office, Donna came in and sat down. This was her normal routine after proofing my presentations.

I asked, "So what do you think?"

"It's hard to imagine that we're that bad," she replied. "We spend so much on all this improvement stuff and you say it's all wrong. How can this be?"

"Good question, Donna." I decided to test my justification on her. "I've asked myself that a hundred times, but let me ask you a question. Is the U.S. winning the war on drugs?"

"No" she said.

"How about gun control, or the war on prostitution?" I probed.

"No," she replied again.

"But yet we continue to spend more and more of our tax dollars on more of the same type of control. I think we do that because our government bureaucracy establishes a philosophy early on, then establishes an infrastructure to support that philosophy, an infrastructure made up of the people in control that have a strong vested interest in maintaining that philosophy." I shrugged. "That's us, except on a smaller scale."

"That sounds evil," she said.

"Not if they really believe it," I said, "which is normally the case." I looked at my watch. "Time to go."

"Do good." She said. "Here are your slides."

I got to the room early to make sure everything was working. I hated it when the damn projection bulb was burnt out. It messed up my tempo, and I typically either burned or cut the hell out of my hand replacing the bulb. I staked out the front left chair, which was right across from where Jack always sat. Everything checked out, and I went outside to the hall. Several of my team were already there.

Vijay said, "So did it all come together? Any surprises?"

"I don't think so, I kept it pretty simple," I said.

Slowly, the principals started arriving. They seemed nice enough, albeit a little on edge. I assumed that since Jack was out of town all week, none had had any discussions with him.

"Hey, Jon. Are you ready?" Jack asked as he wandered into our team gathering.

"Well, hell, yes!" I said, acting indignantly that he'd asked.

He then introduced himself to the team members who didn't already know him, and several were surprised that he remembered them from the distant past. He jokingly gave Jan a hard time because of her husband's third degree. For all his reputation, the man was definitely a people person.

We followed Jack into the room, which became silent as he entered. I'd hoped for a little looser environment. Nathan Jorgenson, who headed Military Products, was in a suit as always. Seated in a row next to Jack were Wayne Tillotson, over Civilian Avionics; Charles Osgood, in charge of Automobile Products; Christine Dumas, who led Security Products. Next to me were Jim Shipmann, over Engineering Services, Kaye Smith, who headed Quality Services, and Peter Winstead, in charge of Purchasing. Doyle Mattingly, our PDSP process czar—the one who had the most to lose—was seated at the end of the table.

Doyle actually reported to Jim Shipmann, but was on the Leadership team because Grant wanted a strong process focus. Actually, I'd never had much respect for Doyle. He was relatively young and had come up through the management fast track program. He hadn't had enough project time to have any real success and had jumped on the process bandwagon as his vehicle for promotion and esteem.

Wayne and Christine were relatively new in their jobs. Both had solid technical reputations. Peter had wanted more involvement from key suppliers for years. *He should be behind my recommendation,* I thought. I really didn't know the others well. I suspected that Nathan and Charles, along with Doyle, would be the vocal opposition.

Jack went to the front of the long table and put the slide from last week that showed our growing profit and market share problems back on the overhead. I was glad he showed this slide again, since it was the basis for my 'new direction' proposal. I just hoped he didn't promise too much before he turned the meeting over to me.

The master of pregnant pauses, Jack slowly made his opening comments. "Last week I showed you this chart, giving the reasons we need to change. It appeared to me that the idea of change ran counter to the general mood of that meeting. You'll recall, I also asked Jon Stevens to lead a team to at least understand the issues and to suggest things we might do differently to reverse these trends quickly. Anyone have any thoughts they want to share before Jon gives us his report."

I thought, *Good, he didn't promise too much.* I hated the pressure when I was over-introduced for a presentation

Doyle said, "Jack, it appears that all of our initiatives, PDSP, Six Sigma, CAD/CAM, business process reengineering, are all intended to address these trends. None of these initiatives are fully deployed. We still have a big change management issue, and that's to convince everyone they have to get on the bandwagon. It looks like the problem is compliance, not the initiatives."

Jack seemed to think for a couple of seconds. Then he said, "Doyle, isn't that what the Soviet Union said for decades about communism? You might be right, but after many years with these initiatives, I see no sign of reversal. In fact, they're a major driver of our engineering overhead rate. The time for wishful thinking has passed. Anything else?"

Not surprisingly, there were no more comments. Jack nodded to me and sat down.

I introduced my team one at a time and thanked them for their effort. Before I was done, I noticed someone new in back, someone who had to be Lori's replacement, and whose name I could not remember. Suddenly, my entire focus was on remembering her name. I didn't want to embarrass her. Luckily, at the last moment it hit me, "and there is Robin Liebermann who is sitting in for Lori Dunlap." That was close. Robin seemed to sense my problem and appeared slightly amused. I put up my first slide (Figure 6a).

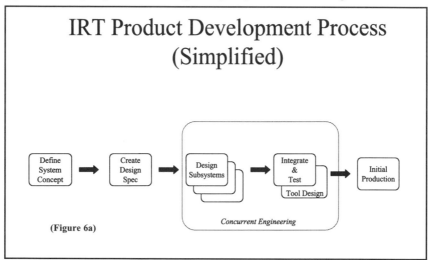

(Figure 6a)

It was intended to acknowledge our process focus and to gain agreement about the scope of product development and our change focus.

"This is a high level snapshot of our product development process. We begin with our customer requirements, develop a system concept around those requirements, create system specifications, and design our subsystems and components. This leads to integration and testing, tool design, and initial production. I think this is an adequate representation as to what we do. Agreed?"

Good old Doyle jumped in as if on queue, clearly intending to establish his credibility as the process expert. "It's mostly correct based on the PDSP model. Tool design and initial production are not really a part of product development. They're actually part of manufacturing, but the flow is okay."

I loved it when I was able to respond to a question and further my own agenda. Maybe if I just shut up and let Doyle talk for a while my job would be really easy. Doyle was either questioning my knowledge or cleverly making the point that manufacturing might be a good part of our problem. Probably it was the former.

I replied, "Be careful, Doyle, you're falling into a trap. I know the PDSP defines the tooling tasks as a part of manufacturing. That's because the PDSP is primarily laid out along organizational lines. But tool design and initial production are part of the product development process."

Doyle said, "So, are you suggesting that all tool designers and some parts of manufacturing report into Engineering?"

"Why would I do that? I thought we'd separated 'the process' from 'the organization.' Remember, product development is the process, or the value-added work. Where people report ought to be determined by where they can best maintain their technical excellence."

Doyle shrugged.

From the back of the room, Robin, our new team member, gave me a 'thumbs-up.' I'd have liked that kind of enthusiasm from everyone.

I put up the next slide to illustrate our product development accomplishments (Figure 6b). I wanted to reiterate that these artificial achievements didn't necessarily relate to the bottom line.

I glanced at the slide and continued. "We've been quite acclaimed for our product development capability. We won the National Quality Award a few years ago, which was for our entire process focus. Our product development initiatives were certainly a key part. We're also probably the most benchmarked company for our size in the country on all of these capabilities. Clearly, we're successful in marketing our processes. On the surface, it would seem illogical for a company with such recognized capabilities to be struggling from a business perspective. Understanding this was an important challenge for our team."

Product Development Capability

- ## Won the National Quality Award
  - Process Focused
- ## Highly benchmarked for
  - Six Sigma Implementation
  - Process Standardization (PDSP)
  - Design Automation (CAD/CAM)

  (Figure 6b)   - Design for Manufacturability

I wasn't surprised that there were no comments on this slide. A couple of people glanced over at Jack, probably to see if there was some indication that maybe things were not as bad as his chart made them seem.

I put up the next slide, hoping to convey that our philosophy was the problem, not our individual managers (Figure 6c). To do this, I needed a simple way of showing the difference.

"Unfortunately, our process is not operationally as clean as it may have looked earlier. There is this rework, or redesign cycle, that almost always happens and is never planned. When it loops back one cycle, it causes serious problems in unplanned costs, confusion, and lost time. A loopback over two cycles probably quadruples the impact, and a loopback to the initial concept is a disaster. It happens way too often."

Nathan Jorgenson challenged this. "Jon, you obviously don't

understand product development. That's the way it works everywhere. As our engineers see better ways to do things, they feel obligated to make the improvements. I don't see that as a problem."

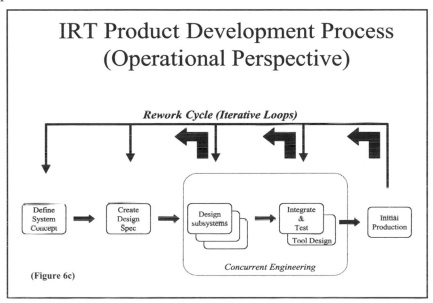

IRT Product Development Process (Operational Perspective)

Rework Cycle (Iterative Loops)

| Define System Concept | Create Design Spec | Design subsystems | Integrate & Test / Tool Design | Initial Production |

Concurrent Engineering

(Figure 6c)

Doyle jumped in before I could respond. "And as I was saying earlier, once everyone follows the PDSP process, these loopbacks, as you call them, will be minimized or eliminated."

I'd hoped to remain calm, civil, and controlled, but I didn't like being talked down to. I believed that both were trying to discredit my credentials for leading this team.

"I disagree with both of you. Nathan, we all know that product development is an iterative learning process, but you don't schedule, budget, or assign resources as though it is. You continually deceive yourself based on the assumption that it's a straight-line process and the iterations can be constrained to a defined cycle. And Doyle, you are being unrealistic if you think any amount of adherence to the PDSP process will somehow eliminate this problem."

Without waiting for a response, I proceeded to the next slide (Figure 6d).

Pointing at this new chart, I said, "The first bullet reiterates what we were just talking about. In product development, the design teams naturally react to what was learned in the prior step. The results from one step drive the actions of the next step. Our linear task-based scheduling system doesn't handle these types of uncertainties well."

The Fundamental Problem

- Product development by its nature is a 'reactive' process, and can not be managed as if it is 'transactional'.

- Our high level of process structure provides an illusion of control that deceives us into thinking that we are better than we are.

(Figure 6d)

Charles Osgood, in his typical bullying style, challenged. "But that is the nature of the beast. We've always done it this way, and we've made a lot of money using our 'task-based' systems, as you call them. And we're good at developing our project plans. You people in manufacturing also use the same system, I might add." He leaned back with a self-satisfied smile.

I personally disliked this man. Whereas many at his level had made it because of their polish and political savvy, Charles was pure intimidation.

Before I could respond, Doyle jumped in with a PDSP commercial. "Also, we're close to having an automatic project scheduling system developed by simply tailoring the PDSP activities to the customer requirements."

It was hard not to take this personally, but I knew I must stay calm and in control. "Charles, just because we make great looking logical project schedules doesn't mean they represent reality. The fact is, they're seldom around at the end of the project. I've never seen a project executed like the plan. We seldom complete a project on time according to the original plan. How can you call that a good system? It's simply what you know. We haven't had any alternatives. And Doyle, you are spending lots of money to automate a system that doesn't meet our needs. That makes a lot of sense." I tried not to sound too sarcastic as I continued. "One more thing, Charles: A task-based scheduling system works in manufacturing because manufacturing is a task-based environment. We should match the tools to the process, not the other way around."

Charles just shook his head to indicate I was wrong, and he was not going to waste any more of his time arguing. I felt my skin crawl. I could tell by looking at the group I was aggravating only Charles, Nathan, and Doyle. The others seemed to be listening intently. Jack, as usual, just listened calmly. He only interrupted if he didn't understand. I knew he'd wait until the end to summarize. He seemed to be enjoying the discussion—certainly more than I was.

I continued while pointing at my second bullet statement. "This discussion illustrates my second point. Our rigid scheduling system creates an illusion of control that deceives us into thinking we're on schedule when we aren't. Likewise, our PDSP process documentation makes us believe that we have a world class process. But do we really? We believe that structure and documentation provides excellence. Luckily, so do most of our competitors."

I quickly changed slides in order to shut off discussion, and kept on talking (Figure 6e).

"The curve on the left is our desired funding profile, the one that would be generated by our scheduling system if it worked. The curve on the right is how it usually looks. It's caused by the unplanned loopbacks we discussed. Strange how we always seem amazed and indignant when the inevitable happens. Doyle, I'm sure your automated system will create a beautiful staffing profile like the one on the left that we'll propose to customers and use to organize resources, but it will seldom if ever happen that way."

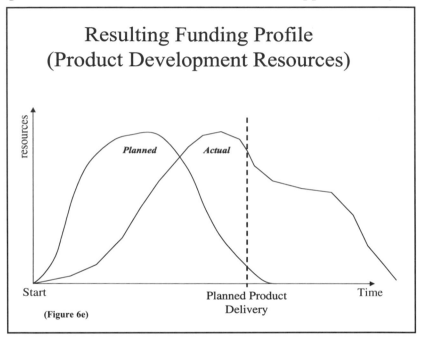

Wayne Tillotson said, "We've actually tried to build some uncertainty into our resource planning and budgets, but our systems don't allow it since we can't justify it. Jon, I don't know how to do any of this differently, but I for one believe that what you're saying is true." I didn't know Wayne well, so I curbed my impulse to go over and hug him for this first sign of support.

Charles said, "Achieving the curve on the left is a matter of resource allocation, not our system or structure. Our functional managers don't provide us with the resources as planned and that causes delays, and so on. That's the primary problem."

Delighted he'd opened the door for me, I said, "Our team had a discussion about one project where we'd actually forced the staffing plan to match the first part of the left curve. The end result was a curve that still looked like the one on the right but with a higher amplitude. I don't remember the project name. Do you remember Dick?"

Dick said, "That was the MIR-48 program. Charles, you should remember that. It was in your business unit at the time."

Charles said, "The problem with that program was bad management."

"Maybe," I replied, "but it sounds like a case of wishful thinking to me. I suspect that there were too many people doing too many premature tasks generating confusion and lots of rework. Regardless of the reasons for that project's problems, our structural processes support the curve on the right. Why would we expect something different?"

Charles leaned back in his seat, some of his smugness gone.

I put up the next slide, thinking this was when the real problems would begin. I knew that everyone would believe I was attacking our initiatives (Figure 6f).

Fatal Issues / Initiative Impact

	6 Sigma	Process Standardization	Design automation
Administrative Leadership	I	--	0
Low value added effort	I	0	0
Ineffective design reviews	0	--	0
Pseudo concurrent engineering	I	--	0
Minimal learning between projects	0	0	I
Low engineering experience	I	0	0
Inaccurate scheduling	0	I	0
Long design loop backs	0	0	0

R = resolves   I = Improves   0 = no change   -- = makes worse   **(Figure 6f)**

I covered the right side of the chart with blank paper. "I've already discussed a couple of issues resulting from our approach to product development. This is a more complete list our team defined in order to pinpoint our problems. We believe all of them must be resolved." I walked through each of the issues just as the team had discussed them, but with only sufficient detail for understanding. Amazingly little disagreement was offered up, except for the continuing notion that this was simply the nature of product development.

Jim Shipmann did say, "Jon, I think we have good concurrent engineering. Why do you call it a problem?"

I said, "Our version of concurrent engineering is based on a consulting paradigm. We place experts on manufacturability, Six Sigma, or whatever on teams to advise designers on what's good or bad. When we looked at this we agreed, however, that true concurrent engineering is when all the perspectives are considered equally from the start of the project. At IRT, we always begin our designs with an engineering perspective on systems performance. Why not begin with a manufacturing perspective on cost?"

Jim said, "From a purist standpoint, I agree. But your paradigm seems too theoretical. We need to be careful that we don't establish unworkable targets as our improvement goals."

I then removed the blank paper. "Before looking at other options, our team did a logical evaluation of current initiatives to determine their ability to resolve the issues. This is the result."

Surprisingly, I didn't get the backlash I'd expected. Some discussion took place on rankings, but most agreed that if these were the issues, our current initiatives wouldn't resolve them. The concern was they'd never be fully resolved in product development. Most felt improvement was the best we could expect.

Without more discussion, I put up my next slide, which introduced them to Toyota's capabilities (Figure 6g).

"It appears most of you believe it's inevitable that the issues just discussed will exist, at least to some degree, and that they'll continue to impact on profits. Well, here's some food for thought.

Toyota and its primary supplier, Nippondenso, don't have those issues. None of them. They also have outstanding business results."

Jack spoke for the first time. "Last week in Detroit with the automakers, I was told that Denso was looking at infrared technologies. We'd better not assume that they're not a future competitor."

Food for Thought

IRT		Toyota / Denso
~20%	Value-added	~80%
Low	Design reuse	High
Slowest	Time to market	Fastest
No	Consistent ROI	Yes

(Figure 6g)

I said, "Their eighty percent value-added number for their engineers is amazing to me, and again, that means that eighty percent of their labor is actually spent developing product. As I understand it, even their supervisors are above eighty percent. In my opinion, there's no way we can compete with a company that is four times more productive doing design work."

"How do we know all of this?" asked a surprised Christine Dumas.

"Because we were part of a consortium organized by the National Center for Manufacturing Sciences that learned this over a several year project."

Christine looked around. "Why did we not hear of this?"

I quickly answered. "The information was presented to various steering committees and was either rejected or ignored for whatever reasons, none of which was because the information was inaccurate or irrelevant. I'd assume it didn't fit the agenda of the steering committee. The same thing happens to a lot of our benchmarking information." I couldn't resist glancing at Doyle, who'd chaired that committee. I decided against sharing that. My point had been made. I couldn't help but notice a smile on Jan's face.

I put the next slide on the overhead projector and continued (Figure 6h).

Toyota / Denso Does Not:

- ## Have a standard detailed product development process
- ## Have a defined Six Sigma initiative
- ## Have an integrated standard CAD/CAM strategy

(Figure 6h)

"Not only do these companies not suffer from our issues while enjoying exceptional business performance, they also don't have a detailed documented product development process like the PDSP. The chief engineers have simple one-page process sheets that define timeframes and integrating events. They don't have a large top-down strategy for Six Sigma implementation. Nor do they have a standardized CAD/CAM initiative with standards for automated integration—although their individual engineers certainly use CAD tools. I don't want to imply that these initiatives are necessarily bad. They just aren't critical to success in Toyota's and Denso's case."

Jim Shipmann, who'd been listening with his typical scowl, interrupted, "I don't understand how they cannot have process standards. Surely everyone can't do whatever he or she wants. That'd be chaos. My impression is that Toyota engineers are very disciplined. I'm confused."

I said, "I don't mean to imply that they don't have documentation or standards. Their standards and documentation have to do with product performance, primarily at the subsystem level—things like tradeoff curves and problem reports."

Jim obviously wasn't satisfied. "Can you be more specific?"

Whenever I gave a technical presentation, one concern I always had was that someone would ask a technical question I wasn't prepared for. This could be embarrassing for a Senior Fellow. Now was one of those times. We hadn't forced Jan to go into a lot of detail on Toyota's standards, and I wasn't the type who could tap dance well around questions I didn't know the answer to.

From the back of the room, Jan jumped in, "Jon, do you mind if I respond to this?"

"No. Go right ahead," I answered, feeling a strong sense of relief.

Jan stood. "My name is Jan Morris. I was our representative on the NCMS project that studied the Toyota system. I'd like to spend a few minutes discussing Toyota's approach to standards. It is diametrically opposed to ours. We have multiple layers of process procedures, but our engineering analyses are really engineer and project dependent. Most of the results are kept in personal engineering and project files. Our design reviews, as we discussed earlier, mostly center on whether or not the tasks were done and when, as opposed to a critical look at the analysis itself." She caught her breath and continued. "Toyota, on the other hand, has very simple process documentation, but stringent standards at the product detail level. We focus on how to do things. Toyota focuses on design results, both what works and what doesn't work. They use standard formats for analysis and prototyping results at the component and subsystem level. They have extensive trade curves that map performance capabilities. All engineers know how to use them and are judged on how well they use them. The knowledge is stored in common functional areas for use across projects. Also, all resolved problems are documented in a prescribed format and distributed in a very formal way. In reality, I'd say they actually have more procedural discipline than we do, only it's centered on capturing knowledge, not process techniques. Hope that helps."

"Thank you, Jan," I said. I thought to myself that she was going to be a CEO somewhere someday. I hoped it would be IRT. In any case, she has just saved my butt.

I looked at Jim. "Okay?" I asked.

He nodded.

Kaye Smith, who headed Quality Services, said, "And they really don't care about Six Sigma?"

"They care tremendously about quality," I responded. "But they don't have a formal Six Sigma program that highlights it. From a statistical perspective, and as a metric, they might use the calculations, which would seem logical. But using Six Sigma strategies as a formal way of improvement is what they don't do. I suppose one could argue that they have a strong Six Sigma culture without formalizing it."

I put up my slide on conclusions. I'd decided not to go into the details on how Toyota works (Figure 6i).

I summarized, "Over the years, IRT has become increasingly more rigid with respect to standards and procedures. It certainly could be argued that this was necessary to get us this far. But we've reached a point where adding more structure seems counterproductive. We need to find a way to hold on to the gains we've made while we refocus on technical excellence and responsibility. Until we do this, we simply cannot be competitive with companies like Toyota that have a totally different philosophy toward product development."

Conclusions

- IRT is not competitive with the best.
- Our increasingly-structured product development environment is becoming counterproductive.
- A new paradigm for product developmer is needed and can be achieved using a knowledge-based approach similar to Toyota's.

(Figure 6i)

The next slide was logically connected, so I put it up and continued (Figure 6j).

Development Environment
- The foundation for lasting change -

A Continuum

Structure-based	Knowledge-based
The basis of the engineering environment is the *structure of the operational activities*: procedures, control, compliance, related training	The basis of the engineering environment is the *knowledge of individual workers*: understanding of needs, information availability, responsibility, and teaming interaction
(IRT Today)	
(Figure 6j)	(Toyota)

"In contrast to our controlling environment, Toyota and Denso rely on the knowledge of the workforce and their ability to capture and share rapid cycles of learning. This is the basis of their product development environment. All of Toyota's structure is focused on increasing and maintaining that knowledge. Their products emerge from the interaction of shared learning."

Nathan Jorgenson led the attack. "I think you just told us to throw away all of our improvement programs, the PDSP process, and all related operational standards, and then just tell our people to go forth and be smart, and the products will simply emerge. Am I reading this right?"

I looked around the room. Anger was apparent in the faces of Nathan, Doyle, and Charles. The rest of the leadership team looked somewhat confused. My team showed concern. But as usual, nothing showed on ol' poker-faced Jack. I knew the next few minutes would be critical and told myself to stay cool.

I decided to dig myself in deeper. "Nathan, believe it or not, even though you were mocking me, you're pretty close. I'm not advocating abandoning all our structure. Some structure is good. Hopefully the right amount could make us the future benchmark ahead of Toyota. What I am advocating is a change in direction— toward less structure and more individual responsibility. I'm concerned as to how far and how fast we should go in changing. This chart shows a continuum between two extremes. There's no doubt we're on the far left and Toyota's on the far right. I'm suggesting that we stop moving farther to the left and start moving to the right. I think the problems before us are how to define the correct level and how to manage the change. This company is stifling under our management and control philosophy. It's time to move to a higher level of performance."

Christine piped up. "Jon, I actually like the premise, I think, but it's so different. There has to be something for us to grab onto in order to change. How do we start?" She seemed genuinely interested and genuinely concerned.

"Christine, our team was struggling with the same question when our time ran out, but let me move into one more layer of detail that I think will give a glimpse as to how it might work."

Quickly, I put up the next slide showing the four key elements of the knowledge-based approach (Figure 6k).

"These are the four key building blocks that must be put in

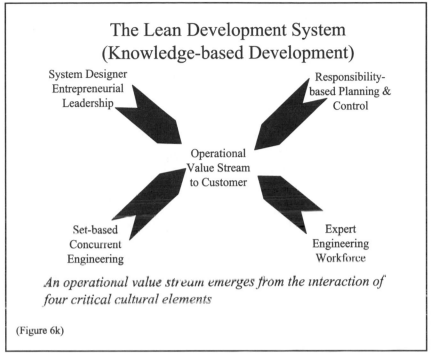

The Lean Development System
(Knowledge-based Development)

System Designer
Entrepreneurial
Leadership

Responsibility-
based Planning &
Control

Operational
Value Stream
to Customer

Set-based
Concurrent
Engineering

Expert
Engineering
Workforce

An operational value stream emerges from the interaction of
four critical cultural elements

(Figure 6k)

place to achieve the knowledge-based environment. This is not
Toyota exactly. It's what researchers determined from studying
Toyota's practices. They identified them as the cornerstones that
will pull the rest of the environment. They're easy to understand,
and they're concrete. Our team spent quite a bit of time discussing
each. We endorse these principles and believe we can build on
them to achieve something significant. Set-based concurrent
engineering is the process for the knowledge-based development
environment. It's much more sophisticated, but in many ways
simpler than our top-down process outlined earlier. It allows
many more alternatives to be investigated earlier, from many more
perspectives, with more innovation, less risk, and with a natural
reuse strategy. To execute this process effectively requires
technical project leadership that places the emphasis on making
design decisions to meet customers' expectations, rather than on
procedural excellence. Project planning and control is based on
key integrating events, design reviews with visible results, and

individual planning and responsibility. All this depends on an engineering workforce with the expertise for design excellence. It will require a shift from top-down administrative leadership to technical coaching. Our team has spent a lot of time on these concepts. They are sound and doable."

I moved quickly to the next slide (Figure 6l). I didn't want to spend a lot of time on details at this point.

	Set-based Process	Engineering Leadership	Responsibility Based Planning	Workforce Expertise
Current Initiative Effectiveness				
Administrative Leadership	I	R	I	0
Low value-added effort	I	I	R	I
Ineffective design reviews	R	R	R	I
Pseudo concurrent engineering	R	0	I	I
Minimal learning between projects	R	0	0	I
Low engineering experience	I	I	I	R
Inaccurate scheduling	0	I	R	I
Long design loop backs	R	I	I	0

R = resolves   I = Improves   0 = no change   -- = makes worse   **(Figure 6l)**

"Our team executed the same logical analysis we did earlier under the assumption that each of these four cornerstones for knowledge-based product development were initiatives."

For the next few minutes, I walked through the reasons why these cornerstones had the potential to resolve our fundamental issues. Amazingly, the comments had more to do with the ability to put them in place than whether they were the right things to do.

Jim summarized what I think everyone was thinking. "Jon, you've made a pretty good case that we need to change. You've given us an overview of something that makes sense, but you haven't given us much detail. I'm concerned that changing direction to this extent might lead to disaster, but I'm also intrigued with the possibilities."

Charles gave his opinion. "Well, I think it's all BS, and we just need to get more aggressive on what we're already doing." This was received by agreeing nods from Nathan and Doyle.

I put up my last slide (Figure 6m).

Final Thoughts / Next Steps

- We have the Toyota validation of Knowledge- based performance gains.
- We have the technology / people.
- We must define an effective change process.
- It just takes commitment.
- We're dead if we do not change.

(Figure 6m)

"What I've tried to do is give you an overview of a different way of looking at product development along with the logic for doing so. I believe I speak for the team when I say that at the highest level of understanding, a knowledge-based process is a better approach for IRT at this time. We believe IRT has the people to pull it off, but that a change process to make it happen has not yet been identified. End of story."

Jack turned to Charles and Nathan and said, "Clearly, Charles, you and Nathan have been critical of these ideas. What are your thoughts?"

After glancing at each other, Charles responded, "I think Jon and his team have some interesting ideas, but I don't think they will work here. We're a different culture. I think we need to accelerate our current initiatives and apply more discipline within the engineering group. We all know that many of our engineers and program managers have never fully bought into our direction. That's where the problem is."

Nathan nodded, and with his all-knowing smirk added, "I agree with Charles. What Jon has proposed is product development chaos. We need more discipline, not less."

Christine said, "Funny you should mention chaos. I read a book last week called *The Minding Organization* that made a very interesting case, at least to me, that highly successful organizations must create deliberate chaos in order to move to emergent order. Otherwise, the result will be to move from deliberate order to emergent chaos. At the time, it made great sense, but I thought it was way too esoteric for us. Jon, it seems that you're proposing the same thing. I can't wait to go back and review the book in this context."

"Who's the author?" I asked. I was intrigued by the possibility that it would corroborate our recommendation. I couldn't help notice the scowls on Charles and Nathan's faces. Christine had defused their argument.

"Moshe Rubinstein, I think was the name, a professor at UCLA, I believe."

Jack said, "Anybody else have thoughts?"

Wayne, who'd been rather quiet, took a turn. "The issues Jon brought up are right on. We all have to admit that. I don't agree with Charles, and I don't understand what Christine said. But I do know it's our best engineers and program managers that are balking at our current initiatives. That's always bothered me. In my opinion, we're in a situation where we're being forced to do something. Frankly, I'm scared, but somewhat excited about the knowledge-based approach. Can we afford, monetarily or emotionally, to launch another new effort, or another program of the year? Plus this is clearly a major change in direction—could end up being a disaster. At least our current initiatives provide some stability. It'd be better if we could just resteer them a bit."

I said, "Wayne, I appreciate your concern." He'd given me an opening to make an important point. "But I have to caution you that this is not a new program. This is a new paradigm or philosophy that will, in my opinion, replace the future need for new and expensive programs of the year. This continuous parade of new improvement programs has generally just added new layers of structure to fix what didn't work—like gun control laws. I hope you appreciate the difference."

"Actually, I do," he said. "Thanks for the clarification."

After allowing a few more minutes of discussion, Jack walked to the front of the room, indicating his intent to close debate and summarize. "I would like to thank Jon and his team. I asked them to be bold and they have been. Frankly, I didn't expect much in such a short time. Ray is pushing hard to bring in a large consulting firm to lead this, and he's my boss. However . . . "He paused. "After hearing this presentation, I believe that course of action would only add more structure and might even be counter-productive. We don't need another layer of control. I'm also very nervous about what seems to be such a major change. I have to wonder about our ability to pull it off. Jon, I'm meeting with Ray and the president of the consulting firm on Friday. Could you and your team please work the change issue? Specifically, if I'm going to bet the company, convince me that the odds are in my favor."

"Sure," I said, but I must admit that I had no clue how to give him those odds.

Jack continued. "We need to reconvene on Thursday at nine o'clock. Let's take a short break. I need the leadership team back in fifteen minutes. Jon, thanks again to you and your team."

My team was waiting outside. All of them were saying nice job, but I never knew whether to believe anyone after a presentation. Who'd ever tell you if you made a lousy pitch.

"Well, is everybody game for another day?" I asked, "I'll understand if you can't." I was pleased they all agreed. "Let's meet in the morning, same place, at eight o'clock. I'm going to play golf this afternoon. Time for a short break."

Dick said, "You talked me into it. My program already thinks I'm out of touch until next week. When's tee time? Besides, we can spend some time talking about the change process."

Golfers can almost always rationalize a round of golf.

"One o'clock at Royal Pines," I said. "Come on."

Tim said he'd like to join us. I turned to leave and realized I'd just created the foursome from Hell. Troy would be there, and he and Dick. . . oh well.

Robin touched my arm to get my attention, introduced herself, and thanked me for allowing her to attend—and for remembering her name. She seemed as eager as Jan had been reluctant. "I think I have an idea that will solve your change problem and maybe also prove that your knowledge-based approach is right." Suddenly she started to look like an angel. She continued. "Do you mind if I try and put something together for tomorrow?"

"Mind? I'd be delighted. We need some new ideas."

Robin then asked whether there was anyone she could work with today to better understand the details of the knowledge-based approach. Luckily Jan walked by.

"Jan," I said. "Do you mind working with Robin this afternoon? She has some ideas about change, but needs background."

"Let me get this straight. You guys are going to play golf while the women stay at home and work, right?" Before I could think of an appropriate comeback, she said, "Sure, I'd be glad to." Turning to Robin and extending her hand, "My name's Jan Morris."

"By the way Jan," I said as I left, "thanks for the save on that question. Good answer."

"You're welcome, and thanks." She smiled. "But you were much too nice to Doyle." She and Robin walked off together in the direction of the cafeteria.

I wondered if I'd just created a two-headed monster.

Back at my office I debriefed Donna, as had been our ritual for years. I decided I'd just surprise Troy when Dick showed up at the golf course. Dick, too. That game might prove to be tougher than the meeting I'd just survived. I decided I needed to keep reminding myself I was retiring.

DISCUSSION

For successful change, a clear leader must exist who demands with a sense of urgency that the change process move forward. This individual must be willing to commit the resources required for success. I have seen excellent potential changes derailed too often by management that doesn't understand, is too easily influenced by company lobbyists, or simply delegates authority to a place where it gets swallowed by administrative overhead. A major change requires a leader who can and will demand the changes. Otherwise, any change that requires major organizational realignments will not survive.

The leader can have the vision for change, can lead the discovery effort for the new vision, or be willing to adopt a vision created by others. In the IRT example, Jack assigned responsibility to his most trusted technical advisor and surrounded that advisor with capable resources. Jack understood that he would not be in a position to accept recommendations requiring major changes if he was to institute anything less than a fully-supported effort by his most trusted helper. Moreover, acceptance of a new vision for operations will almost always require significant engineering intuition as justification.

Illustrated in the IRT case study are four key attributes for success.

1. The leader must be willing to commit.

On many occasions I've seen teams formed to make improvements, although it was obvious that the leader would never actually commit to the necessary changes. The team would often settle on somewhat trivial solutions they believed would gain commitment.

2. The leader must understand.

At the very least, the leader must understand the major issues, risks, and the impact of moving ahead. He or she must also have confidence in those developing the details of the change. Without understanding and trust, any commitment will be weak at best.

3. The leader must be willing to act.

Too often, I've seen leaders tacitly accept proposals simply by not stopping the funding of them. That low level of commitment will not support major change. The leader must communicate boldly, must be willing to assign the best resources, must demand aggressive milestones, and must stay involved. Change initiatives always have significant opponents who search for ways to undermine the effort. A wavering leader gives them an easy target.

It's not reasonable or advisable to expect a one-time commitment to major change. Commitment must grow over several steps of the process. Commitment to action is followed by acceptance of the vision, assignment of change resources, and active involvement in the actual change process. Passive leadership for major change projects is simply not acceptable.

In the IRT example, Jack committed to the vision with strong reservations about the lack of a change plan.

4. The leader must be willing to let go.

There's a slight but important distinction between this statement and one that says the leader must be willing to take risks. Taking risks is macho. Think about it. Would you want to be an employee whose leader took risks with your livelihood?

The book *The Minding Organization* argues that development must move from deliberate chaos to achieve emergent order. In other words, the leader needs to set the high level vision but no more. This deliberately creates a state of pending change, whereas a leader who sets the vision and then follows this with implementation details has deliberately created a state of perceived order. This, according to the book and my experience, will inevitably lead to a state of chaos followed by long, expensive, and only marginally successful efforts to eliminate the chaos. On the other hand, good results can readily be achieved if the organization is allowed to realize the vision in its own way.

It has been my experience that the creativity required to achieve any corporate vision exists throughout an organization. It is not to be found solely in the minds of a few. The vision sets the stage. The leader must understand this and trust that the desired results will emerge. His or her role is to be true to the vision and demanding of results.

Chapter 7

Defining the Transition
(The Power of Involvement)

The details of the new organizational environment are the heart of the changes. They define new roles, new opportunities, and threaten the status quo of organizations and personal responsibilities. The challenge is to align personal expectations and goals with the organizational vision.

Tuesday morning, Infrared Technologies Corporation

I overslept and didn't arrive at the plant until about 7:30 on Tuesday morning. I was hoping that Jan and Robin had been successful in discovering some semblance of a change plan. I'd gone into the plant after our golf round to find some old slides and ended up in an interesting discussion with Donna about change. The lady did get involved. I didn't sleep well because I had way too much to think through.

Upon reflection, I'd decided that Jack really wanted to buy in, but needed more confidence that what we had proposed was possible. We only had today to figure out how.

Greg was waiting by my office, talking to Donna when I arrived. I thought maybe he had some sort of change vision that would make everything work. He and Donna followed me into my office and sat down.

"How was the golf game?" Greg asked. "Did they kill each other?"

It's amazing how much more interesting interpersonal relations are than business issues.

"It was the most intense three dollar Nassau game I have ever played," I said, honestly.

"What's a Nassau game?" Donna asked.

"It's three matches. We play by hole, best ball wins, for the front nine, back nine, and the entire eighteen holes."

"So why is it called that?" she said.

Since I had no clue, I shrugged. "Dick and Tim played Troy and me—engineering versus manufacturing. The longest putt given all day was about six inches. Troy and I started winning on the back nine and they started pressing."

Donna asked, "What does that mean?"

"It means that whenever one team is behind, they can start a new bet for the remaining holes. They were pressing their presses. It came down to the final hole, and I had a three foot putt which would decide it all."

Donna said, "And?"

"I hit a good putt but it didn't break, and we lost."

"You mean you choked! So, how much did you lose?"

I shook my head. As usual no sympathy would be forthcoming from Donna. "Four bucks, and I didn't choke."

She turned and muttered over her shoulder as she left, "All that intensity over four bucks? Men are strange."

I turned to Greg. "What's really strange is that afterwards, over a round of beers, Troy and Dick became friends."

"No way."

"We started reminiscing," I said, "and they both realized how much they disliked the same people. They seemed to bond over their common prejudices. Come on, we need to get to the meeting."

When we arrived, Jan and Robin were sitting together at the front of the room sorting slides. They seemed to be in a good mood. I didn't know whether that was good or bad. After a few minutes spent discussing our uncertainty as to how the presentation had gone, I went to the front of the room to set the stage.

Before I began, Jan asked, "So how was the golf game?"

"Just great," Dick answered. "Our leader choked on a two foot putt to lose all the money on the last hole."

After a few minutes of fun at my expense, Carl thankfully changed the subject. "I went by Christine's office to get that book that she mentioned, *The Minding Organization*, but she'd already loaned it out."

"To Jack, right?" I said.

"Right," Carl said. "How'd you guess?"

"Because he's looking for verification." I said. "He always does that. Damn, I have to find and read that book by tomorrow."

Carl said, "Here it is. Have at it. I bought it on the way home and read it last night." He seemed pleased with his effort. "The book is amazing as to its correlation with the Toyota environment. In my opinion, it defines the academic theory, and Toyota is the proof. The authors even used a car example that proposes what Toyota actually does. They never mention Toyota. I'm not sure they were aware of the similarities."

I said, "Thanks. I've learned never to go into a meeting where Jack's leapfrogged me in knowledge. He loves to do that."

I paused, looked around the room and said, "Before I turn our meeting over to Jan and Robin, I want to say a few words to set the stage. We know our challenge. We have to understand today how to change our product development process from a structural, linear, task-based process to one in which products emerge from the collective learning and knowledge of the engineering workforce. There's a huge gap between the two systems that will be difficult to cross. I suspect from your expressions that you lack confidence in our ability to do this." After a pause, I continued. "I had an interesting conversation yesterday afternoon with Donna, my opinionated, but intuitive assistant. She made a few observations I'd like to share. I was discussing how hard this transition was going to be. After a few minutes, she stopped me and asked a question, which was this: If you took a poll of all of the engineering workforce as to whether they'd rather work in a structural, command and control environment, or in a learning environment based on their collective knowledge and experience, what would the results be?

"Then she answered her own question. She believed the results would be highly in favor of the change. Yet, manager types, as she called us, for some reason think the change would be difficult. It seemed to her that the problem was not changing the people, but rather keeping management and policies out of the way."

I paused to let this sink in, then continued. "I couldn't answer her, and I will swear that if we fail this morning to define a change plan, I'll bring her in this afternoon. Then we'll all try to answer her. With that said, I'll turn it over to Jan and Robin."

"Thanks, Jon," Jan said. "You really know how to put pressure on. I don't think I'd want to answer to Donna on that. In the NCMS project, we evaluated the cultural differences between highly-structured companies, like IRT, and less-structured, like Toyota, but from a different perspective. I think it supports your position, and Donna's. We created a capability assessment form for all the companies on the consortium. All except Toyota were about the same. This is the comparison between structural companies and Toyota." She put up another slide (Figure 7a).

"Notice the large differences between us and Toyota on some rather fundamental characteristics. By the way, all of the consortium companies were aligned almost exactly with IRT on this chart. To me, this says that it's logical to assume that a structural push environment will create organizational characteristics over time like ours, but a knowledge-based environment will pull a completely different set of organizational behaviors similar to Toyota's." Jan used a pointer to scan the chart. "For example, any company that's based on procedural control will tend toward administrative program management, and any company like Toyota that's based on technical learning or

Organizational Capability Assessment Form
(Toyota ● vs Traditional (IRT) ◆)

← *Range* →

Program Management

Administrative Based
(Totally concerned with budgets, schedules, resources, admin issues)

Engineering Based
(Totally concerned with technical issues: decision making, customer interface, resource leadership)

Teaming Style

Interfaced
(One-on-one communication as needed to resolve issues; otherwise through interface agreements)

Highly Interactive
(Totally open teaming as people perceive need; high degree of spontaneity; little formality)

Project Information Sharing

Guarded
(Keep information to oneself; push to others as you perceive they need it)

Concurrent
(Project information available and easily accessible for all; a way of life)

Project Engineering Proficiency

Entry level
(Design engineers are mainly junior level with little experience)

Highly Experienced
(Design engineers mainly are highly experienced & functionally skilled)

Cross Project Learning

Ad-Hoc
(Learning across project is based on informal sharing as resources move across project)

Ingrained
(learning across projects is systematic and is highly effective)

CAD/CAM Proficiency

Basic
(Product development teams are poorly equipped and inconsistent in technical computer skills)

High
(Product development teams are routinely well equipped and skilled in the application of computer technology to the project: expected)

Corporate Engineering Infrastructure

Minimal
(No infrastructure exists outside projects to support process development, system support, or new technologies)

Extensive
(strong infrastructure exists for systematic development and application of new processes and technologies into projects)

(Figure 7a)

188

knowledge, will almost assuredly have engineering leadership. Just look down the list and you'll see what I mean—teaming style, information sharing, engineering proficiency. You have to admit all of the Toyota characteristics are desirable and seem to be natural extensions of their development philosophy."

I said, "I have to agree with Donna's assessment that most engineers would prefer to operate in the Toyota culture."

Tim said, "Jan, I understand and agree with most of your premise. But I don't understand the CAD/CAM standardization line. Does Toyota believe that design automation isn't important?"

"Actually, it's that we believe it's so important." Jan said. "It's part of what our structure is built on. We use CAD/CAM to enforce standard designs and integration. Toyota only uses it for engineering productivity."

Dennis said, "I assume that the minimal corporate infrastructure at Toyota is driven by their lack of support organizations for standards, computer automation, and other stuff like that."

Jan responded, "Yes, and ours is just the opposite, and growing."

I added, "Which explains part of our growing engineering overhead rate on Jack's chart."

Jan said, "I hope you all agree that this is our challenge for today, to define a plan to close this gap in order to allow the knowledge-based environment to be successful. Here are a couple of interesting questions. If we had this cultural environment, would we also have knowledge-based development? Or, if we forced the knowledge-based environment, would it pull the cultural changes?"

Jan introduced Robin, and she eagerly took the stage. I'm not sure I 'd ever seen someone so into the moment.

"Let me give you a little background on me," she began. "I'm part of the business process engineering team and have been working with Lori on software process improvements. I was originally an engineer supporting the Total Quality Management initiative, so I've been a change agent for a lot of years. And let me tell you, it's been very frustrating dealing with our lack of ability to change. We're too slow to maintain any change momentum and, as a result, we never consistently achieve the gains we target. I'm going to present you with a different way to change which I think can work to create the knowledge-based environment. By the way, I'm considered somewhat a maverick among the others in my group."

Somehow this didn't surprise me.

She continued. "Let me walk through how I view change initiatives at IRT, and at most other large companies. We create a reengineering team, or some sort of elite team or improvement organization. This team defines the new process or change on paper, creates their view of the organizational infrastructure required, and then usually has some sort of pilot to verify that it all works. This pilot is generally successful from the team's perspective, but it's always suspect from the viewpoint of the rest of the organization. This process takes a year at minimum. Okay so far?"

Everybody nodded. We'd all observed many change initiatives following this model.

She said, "Then we spend the next few years trying to convince everyone we were right. We identify the change agents, the sponsors, the targets, and many other names for people involved. We have all kinds of structure as to the technical details of how we convince everyone to follow the new process. We even have our own names for the stages of change. Normally the change just loses momentum and fades away."

We all laughed. She was exactly right. We'd all seen it happen over and over.

She continued. "There've been a lot of documented successes for process reengineering efforts, but mostly in transactional types of business, such as insurance and banking, not a lot of successes in product development environments.

"Now let me discuss some other approaches. One is when the leader of the organization decrees all the changes and uses his power to force compliance. For this to work, the leader must be involved in all parts of the change. This can be very effective with a small company and a visionary leader.

Another approach is a continuous improvement model for change. This is where a strong Six Sigma environment is so great, because its problem-solving methodology, applied on an ongoing basis, can sustain a strong improvement curve. The problem is, you can't really expect any continuous improvement methodology to make breakthrough changes in the organizational culture. The methodology can, however, make dramatic operational improvements. These are the primary modes of change that I know about."

Greg said, "I've seen a number of seminars on applying lean thinking into manufacturing and development. Where does this fit?"

Jan said, "I'd put that in the strong continuous improvement change model. The approach is to define the value stream, then to systematically find and eliminate waste. While I believe that this model—both Six Sigma and lean-based—will be a part of what we recommend, it simply won't change our culture to the degree required. But it will be the way to sustain the gains."

After a few more minutes of discussion, Robin continued her story. "In Boston, there's a business process engineering forum where all the companies come together quarterly to share common practices that have to do with new processes and change methodologies. Last year, I attended a forum as IRT's representative. There was a guy from an oil company presenting his story on how they'd reengineered their 'order fulfillment' process. They'd failed miserably on 'rolling out' the changes to the organization. Then they did it another way and it was totally successful—almost magical were his words. I spent quite a bit of time with him after his presentation so I'd understand the details. He also suggested I attend a conference that was being held a couple of weeks after that, which I did. I'd been trying to figure out what to do with all of this knowledge until yesterday when I heard Jon's presentation. Now I know."

With all this incredible buildup, I decided to take a fifteen-minute break. I wanted to hold onto the illusion for a few more minutes that this exuberant lady really had everything figured out.

As we were leaving, Carl asked Robin if she was this enthusiastic about everything she did.

"Mostly," she said, laughing, "I just hope I can explain it properly."

When we got back, Robin put up a slide that outlined the approach (Figure 7b).

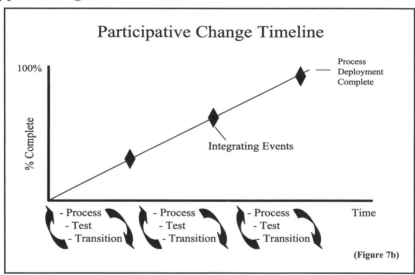

(Figure 7b)

"What I learned by talking to the man at the forum—and subsequently at the conference, which was about 'large group interventions for organizational change'—is that there's a totally different methodology for complex organizational change. In this approach, you don't have a side group of experts that make the decisions. You use large cross sections of the organizations to simultaneously define and make the changes. I'm calling it the participative approach because it involves everyone in the organization. The people doing the actual work are the experts and have the knowledge. You have large integrating events where sub-organizational solutions are combined or eliminated, and new plans made for the next events. Most decisions are made during those events. They're normally spaced about three months apart. Between the events, volunteers from various organizations define and test the changes. Once the new ideas are proven and okayed at the integrating events, the changes are deployed in the way that makes sense within an organization. The new process and environment sort of emerges from the interaction of all the sub-organizations. This is actually a big deal. There were six hundred to a thousand people at the conference, all espousing how successful this approach is for organizational change. There seem to be hundreds of books written on the subject, but it's rarely used in manufacturing companies. I've had very little luck getting my cohorts here to even consider it."

Dick made an observation. "You're obviously drawing the analogy that this 'participative' change approach is like the 'knowledge-based' concept for product development. If I understand correctly, the designs will emerge from the knowledge-based process that itself will emerge from this 'participative' change approach." He touched his temples. "This is hurting my head."

"Think about it," Robin said. "An organizational change is like a new product, albeit in a different vein. It has to be designed, it has to be integrated, it has to be tested, and it has to be made real. Jan and I put this next chart together to show the similarities." With that said, she put up her next slide (Figure 7c).

I was intrigued with her premise. If indeed this 'participative' methodology for change was consistently successful, and if it was analogous to the knowledge-based approach, then this would give more credence to our conclusions about knowledge-based development being inherently superior to point-based. But that was a lot of "ifs."

Robin continued with confidence. "The four principles on the left are the four cornerstones of knowledge-based engineering from your charts. On the right are the important concepts of the participative change process aligned to those principles. In participative change, you build from the bottom with multiple sets of potential solutions and multiple prototypes. In knowledge-based development, you have a chief engineer who makes the integrating decisions either at or in preparation for large project integrating events. Of course, an integrating staff would help. In participative change there's a similar approach, but decisions are generally made at integrating events and are guided by a facilitator using intervention techniques for forcing consensus. Also, in participative change, all planning and control is the responsibility of the people doing the work. It's based on what they've found effective. So the knowledge of the entire workforce is used to define the changes. Jan and I think the two concepts are very much the same. The end result is that the knowledge-based environment will emerge from the interaction of the different organizations."

Analogy
Knowledge-based Development / Participative Change

KBD Principles	*Participative Concepts*
•Set-based Concurrent Engineering	•Build from the Bottom •Multiple Prototypes / Alternatives
•System Designer Leadership	•Leader sets Vision / Integrating Events •Integration Staff
•Responsibility-based Planning & Control	•All key planning / Decisions made by people responsible for results
•Expert Workforce	•Large Group Participation •People Lead •Broad Expertise

(Figure 7c)

194

Carl said, "I hate to bring up *The Minding Organization* again, but it certainly seems to me that this participative approach is in sync with the principles in the book. You start with multiple perspectives and allow the people to work through the organizational change details. Everyone is on board. In effect, all parts of the organization are working to the same mind set."

Robin acknowledged Carl's input. Her next slide continued the emergence analogy (Figure 7d). She waited for our reaction.

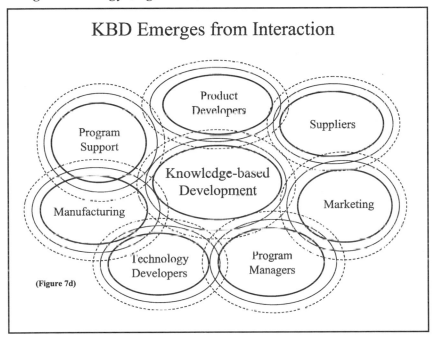

(Figure 7d)

"This chart is the bottom line—we allow the culture required to support the Toyota knowledge-based development philosophy to emerge through the involvement of all of the impacted organizations."

Tim said, "Robin, I must admit your premise is pretty intriguing—to make the change to a knowledge-based development environment using a knowledge-based change approach, but I really don't understand how these integrating events work. How many people are we talking about at these things?"

"It can be anywhere from a hundred to upwards of a thousand

people at the event," Robin said. "For complete buy in, it must be the critical mass of knowledgeable people from the many organizations involved. The large group facilitator knows how to gain consensus on decisions. He or she would have been working with the integrating staff to plan the session. This is obviously more complex than product-level decisions, since there are so many more organizations involved. It'd be dangerous for anyone, even Jack, to make those decisions unilaterally. At this conference, there were many, many testimonials about how well this works. There are a number of excellent consultants who can set up an approach that would work best for us, but again, the key is that the integrating decisions, the planning, and the results are generated by pulling it from the people doing the work—the same as for knowledge-based product development."

I opened my mouth, not knowing exactly where I was headed. "Robin, one of the important points of the knowledge-based approach is the use of set-based concurrent engineering. One of the things I really like about that is the risk mitigation of always having a backup. Show me where I have this in the participative change approach. If you can do that, I think I'll start buying your analogy."

Robin immediately looked to Jan for some help. It seemed obvious she hadn't anticipated my question. Too bad, I'd really been hoping for a good answer.

Jan suggested we break for lunch. Everybody laughed at her for this, but we agreed to have lunch slightly early. I hoped she and Robin would come up with an answer.

After we returned to the room, Robin addressed my question with Jan standing at her side. "Okay, Jon, I think we have an answer. Your question is, how does the participative change approach address the issue of risk reduction through redundancy, if it is indeed analogous to the knowledge-based system. Correct?"

I nodded and she continued. "Something that one of the change consultants told me, that I never did understand, was never to pilot off-line. The changes should be prototyped for real on active projects. I believe that the answer to your question is that the backup for the changes is to continue to do it the same way. The change prototypes are planned at the integrating events, but always on projects where the people involved are confident that they can test the changes with no risk to the project. Their commitment to the change, in addition to their project commitment, will ensure the project success."

Tim nodded his head. "Jon, this is logical," he said. "Since all the changes are created from the bottom up, and since there's always the current way as an alternative, then the changes tested on live programs will offer both low risk and direct comparison of the benefits. For example, one of the fundamentals of the Toyota approach is that the engineers, being the ones responsible, make their own schedules to meet key milestones. We could easily do that in parallel with our traditional top-down schedule, which we all know is generally screwed up anyway. The engineers would love it. Of course, Doyle's process police would hate it."

I must admit I liked the answer, which was fairly straightforward and simple.

Before Robin could start again, Carl slowly rose and walked to the wide chalkboard on the side of the room. "Okay, let me play System Engineer for a few minutes."

Jay said, "Carl, you don't have to play at it. You're probably our best system engineer."

"Thanks." Carl chuckled. "But to be honest, I don't know what I am any more after all this discussion." Holding the marker, but not writing, he continued, "I think we need to test this premise that the change process mirrors the knowledge-based process, and maybe it will help give us more insight into both."

"Go for it, " Robin said, and sat down.

"What are the major subsystems on a car?" Carl asked.

Jay, our mechanical engineer, responded. "Well, there's the engine, the frame, the sheet metal body, and I guess the interior."

"Close enough," Carl said. He wrote on the board.

Auto subsystems
- Frame
- Engine
- Body
- Interior

"So, what are the subsystems of the knowledge-based process?" he asked, although it was clear from his expression he already knew the answer.

Greg bit. "They're the set-based process, the system designer leadership, the expert work force, and responsibility-based planning and control."

"Okay," he said with a smile. He wrote on the board along side the other.

KBD subsystems
- Set-based process
- System designer leadership
- Expert workforce
- Responsibility-based planning and control

"So, are these roughly analogous?" he asked.

"Yeah, to a large extent," Vijay replied. "They all have to be designed. They all have to support the overall system, and they have to be integrated."

Everyone seemed to agree, and Carl pressed on. "So, can we expand each of the KBD subsystems and list the design issues we have to understand and resolve for each? If we can, then I believe that our analogy holds." Without waiting, he went back to the board and broke out each subsystem. "The set-based process—

what are some issues?" After a few minutes of discussion, he listed the following:

Set-based process design issues
- *What are the integrating events?*
- *How are alternatives documented?*
- *How does it impact our information systems?*
- *How do we document our changing specs and agreements?*

"I'm sure there are more issues," Carl added, "but I think these are enough to demonstrate that the set-based subsystem does have its own unique design issues to be resolved. So, what are the issues for the other subsystems?"

After some more brainstorming, Carl had filled the complete board.

System designer leadership
- *Who are they?*
- *How are they organized?*
- *Is it one person, or a small team?*
- *How are they trained, and maintained?*
- *What are their incentives?*

Expert workforce
- *What are the incentives to maintain the expertise?*
- *How are tradeoff curves documented and maintained?*
- *How are tradeoff curves used between projects?*
- *How does the functional mentoring happen?*
- *How are the designers organized?*

Responsibility-based planning and control
- *How are individual plans rolled up?*
- *How are alternatives integrated into the system?*

- How are resources allocated across projects?
- What is the visibility and documentation approach?

Carl concluded, "So far, so good on our analysis. I think it's safe to call these four things subsystems. They have their own issues but only have real significance when combined into the overall KBD system. Okay?"

Everyone nodded in agreement and Greg copied what was on the board.

While erasing the board, Carl said, "Let's talk about project milestones and how they compare with a KBD development project and the participative change project."

"Jan," Carl called out without turning from the board, "What are some key milestones that Toyota uses for developing a car?"

Jan said, "Remember that milestones are defined as key points of natural integration of the system. The importance of that being that it forces decisions and the narrowing of alternatives. Here are some key ones, but there might be more on some projects, depending on the scope of changes—'Vehicle targets, concepts defined.' 'Styling, concept approved,' probably with a clay model. 'Full-scale prototype.' 'First production unit.'"

He wrote them lengthwise on the board, but added the word "Launch" at the first, and asked, "Anyone, what would be corresponding milestones for the change process?" He added a corresponding "Launch" on the change line.

After a few moments, Carl answered his own question. "How about 'KBD system targets / concepts'. There's nothing that says our goals or our concepts have to be like Toyota's, so we ought to get multiple possibilities on the table, in addition to setting our goals and quantifying the targets for change."

Jan concurred. "I like that. On our NCMS project, we had a concept called 'Fast System build' that was a continual simulation approach of rolling up approaches and testing them at the system level. We all liked it conceptually. It was kind of a systematic and fast point-based process with all knowledge based on system impact. This idea, or others like it, could be identified as a part of that milestone."

Tim agreed. "I'm okay with that Carl. So how about the next one being the 'KBD Process Approved,' which would be locking down our version of the set-based process, which would be analogous to the 'Styling / concept approval'. It would seem logical to set the process parameters first before finalizing the other organizational details."

Dick agreed and added, "And the next would be that the entire organizational system is approved, which would include all the subsystems—the set-based process, the system designer approach, the expert workforce, and the responsibility-based planning system. At this milestone, all the issues that we listed above would have been resolved and documented. This seems cleanly aligned with the 'Full Scale Prototype' milestone."

Tim quickly added, "And the last milestone would be the first implementation of the KBD system in one of our business units."

Carl completed aligning the milestones (Figure 7e). He

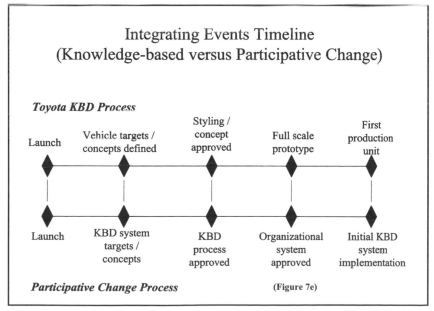

Integrating Events Timeline
(Knowledge-based versus Participative Change)

Toyota KBD Process

| Launch | Vehicle targets / concepts defined | Styling / concept approved | Full scale prototype | First production unit |

| Launch | KBD system targets / concepts | KBD process approved | Organizational system approved | Initial KBD system implementation |

Participative Change Process   (Figure 7e)

stepped back from the board. "Whether these are exactly correct is really not important, but I think the parallels are sufficient for our comparison. Is everyone all right so far?"

Buoyed with only slight concern for the quickness of our analysis, Carl opened up his last issue. "Jan or Robin, it seems like the analogy breaks down in the decision-making and the role of these large-scale events. In the KBD approach there's a chief engineer, or system designer, that makes the overall product-level decisions, and not in the presence of all project personnel, much less a large microcosm of the entire company. It seems that it's expected, in the participative change process, that the key decisions are actually made in these large conference settings. Can one of you comment on this?"

Robin looked over at Jan, and then spoke up. "Ever since we started on this analogy, I've been thinking about that. Actually, we might be breaking new ground here. There really are two separate issues. The first is the need for the large group integrating sessions, and the second is the decision-making. Let me address the need for the large integrating sessions first. In a typical product development project, the number of people involved is relatively small compared to a large cultural change project. In addition, the chain of command on a product development project, and the responsibilities are well defined, controlled, and respected. On a cultural change project, the people involved are neither well-defined and controlled, nor are the results necessarily respected. Being subversive will get you fired on a real project, but is often considered bold and clever when done in the confines of a change initiative. The importance of the large integrating events is to gain broad involvement, understanding, ideas, volunteers, and to maintain change momentum. So, in reality, the large group session for integration is really more of a tactical difference, as opposed to substantive." She leaned back and waited for reaction.

I was okay with her response, but wanted to think more about it. It seemed as though most of us were in tentative agreement.

Robin then addressed the second issue. "In my change world,

for many of the reasons I just mentioned, the concept of an individual directing a change initiative has never played out well. Too often, they have taken on a czar status, with no real checks or balances, and with a resulting seemingly lifelong bureaucratic job.

"Oh, you must know Doyle," Jan said sarcastically.

Robin ignored this comment and plowed ahead. "However, if Jack were to properly assign a well respected chief engineer, or whatever we would call a chief change leader, assign clear responsibilities *and duration*, clear milestones, and with a real mandate, then I think it could work. It might be better if it was a team of two or three and included a well-respected integration team. The large integration meeting could then be more of communication and consensus buy-in than decision-making, although I think allowing some level of decision-making at the integration meetings would be helpful for active involvement. I also think that using these sessions for active planning and obtaining volunteers for prototyping is very important. The more meaningful and dynamic these sessions are, the more attendance and participation will be obtained. I believe that a happy medium could be found."

"Okay, I see your rationale for the large group participation." Carl summarized, "While I do like the approach of using the KBD system to actually make the change, I realize there are some differences with a change project that must be addressed. But I'm confident that a good chief engineer, in charge of the change process, will make it work.

On a whim, I put up one last chart (Figure 7f).

I said, "One thing we don't know is how far we need to go on the continuum from our current environment to knowledge-based. Do we need to go as far as Toyota? It'd seem that the participative approach would allow a natural way to find that point by building from the four cornerstones, rather than designing the processes from the top down."

Robin responded, "Jon, I know that must be a concern because it's so different from what we've seen. However, it is not really going to be that big a problem. Before we ever start, we'll pick the primary consultant for leading the participative change. That consultant, the integration team, and Jack will work together to find the right blend of size and approach. The fact that Jack wants this change and will hold to his vision are the real keys to success."

Development Environment
- The foundation for lasting change -

A Continuum

Structure-based	Knowledge-based
The basis of the engineering environment is the **structure of the operational activities**: procedures, control, compliance, related training **(Figure 7f)**	The basis of the engineering environment is the **knowledge of individual workers**: understanding of needs, information availability, responsibility, and teaming interaction

---

I added my final thoughts. "I agree. Jack is the key. All the participative process does is provide an orchestrated methodology for the workforce to develop its own processes to his vision. That's the way it should be. Any disagreement?"

Carl said, "Actually, again, if you buy into the concepts of that book," he pointed to the copy of *The Minding Organization* he'd passed to me, "then even if the concepts are not perfect, the people will make it work because they're all involved. That's largely the theme of the book."

Everyone was in agreement. Now if I could just explain it properly. I had a day to put the presentation together and had a couple of books to read.

DISCUSSION

The vision of a new system may be fine. But many brilliant ideas for organizational improvement have fallen flat on their faces because of the inability to enact the required change. Not only are there new systems, procedures and tools to learn, there's also the natural resistance to anything new. The traditional change approach is the "convincing model," where a selected team decides on the new structure and attempts to convince the organization of the wisdom of it. The fact is, experts at doing specific tasks resent being told there's a better way by people who have minimal experience doing the same tasks.

I strongly recommend that the participative change approach be used, particularly for a change in the process of product development. As has been discussed, the similarity between this approach to change and knowledge-based development is striking. In addition, the ability to draw upon the broad expertise of the engineering workforce is enhanced by the participative methodology.

Summarizing from the IRT example, the following provides the foundation for the participative methodology for change:

1. Leadership commitment to the change and methodology.

In the participative approach, the organization's leader delegates the change details to those in the functions impacted. The leader sets the vision, ground rules, and change targets, and allows them to define the specifics. This approach for change assumes that the workforce, as opposed to a selected team, has the knowledge and will accept the responsibility to make the correct changes. These assumptions are consistent with the knowledge-based methodology. In the change summary contained in the previous chapter, I stated that the leader must be willing to let go. He or she must trust the workforce to achieve the vision. The leader is placing his trust in the participative process and the affected people to orchestrate the changes. In reality, there is very little risk. Having been given the responsibility, the workforce will make it work.

2. Establish a rapid response timeline.

Also, consistent with knowledge-based development, the participative methodology requires a rigid timeline for completion of the change process. Key milestone dates for major integration events need to be set early in the process. The organization's leader needs to assure that these dates are adhered to.

3. Use the workforce's expertise.

Broad representation from all functions that will be affected is the cornerstone of the participative approach. The representatives are usually volunteers that are willing to participate in the integrating events and to perform prototyping activities in their work areas as defined at the integrating events. It is important for these volunteers to know they have the responsibility for both defining and implementing the required changes within their work groups.

This change methodology requires a strong commitment from the business leadership.

Chapter 8

Committing to Organizational Change
(The Power of Confident Leadership)

Visibly allocating resources to the change process is a strong and necessary commitment from the business leader. Halfway measures, such as a small test program or pilot, will be seen as weak commitment. The eventual success of a major change program will be inversely proportional to the time frame for change.

Thursday morning, Infrared Technologies Corporation

Driving to the plant, I had mixed emotions. After this morning's presentation, I'd be back in retiree-in-waiting mode. My official last day would be in two weeks. I'd enjoyed this assignment more than I'd expected. I really believed that we'd arrived at a good solution, coupled with a change plan that would allow it to work. But I was worried that my presentation detail was not doing it justice. Some of the team wanted to be more involved in the preparation, but since I'd never been able to effectively present other people's material, I'd chosen to build the presentation alone.

After I'd finished it last night, I'd spent about an hour on the phone with Allen Ward. He wasn't familiar with this participative type of change, but he seemed genuinely impressed with its similarities to the knowledge-based approach. I'd also read much of the book on participative change and scanned the notes of proceedings from the large group intervention conference. As Robin had said, this approach had a significant track record for organizational change, and its similarities to the knowledge-based environment for product development were striking. In fact, these documented case studies might be the best examples, outside of Toyota, that a knowledge-based approach is a superior development environment. The approach met all the criteria that Allen had mentioned: many alternatives from many perspectives of the organization, technical leadership through the integration teams, scheduling driven by the results of the integrating events, and broad representation of the people owning the technical expertise.

One of the key issues that both the book and the proceedings identified was the courage and commitment the organization's leader needed to engage in this change process. Any wavering in accepting the participative results would be disastrous to successful change. So it was imperative that Jack not only buy into today's presentation, but that he buy in completely.

I'd also skimmed parts of *The Minding Organization*, wishing I'd had the whole weekend to do both books justice. That one had given me confidence in both the knowledge-based paradigm and the participative approach. Even though the books were written separately, it was amazing how they both came to similar conclusions. I was hoping Jack would see it the same way. I was sure he'd read it more carefully than I had.

It was about eight o'clock when I walked into the plant, an hour before the meeting, and everything was ready. I had even gotten my critique from Donna last night before I'd gone home.

Troy was waiting for me at my office. He must have sensed I was approaching retiree mode again.

"I came by on my way to the cafeteria," he said. "Want to join me?"

"Sure," I said. Drinking coffee and talking golf would be a great way to pass the next hour.

We were heading down the hall and Troy said, "Donna let me see your presentation for this morning. Pretty interesting proposal.

I'm sure Doyle will vote for it."

"Yeah, right," I said, laughing. "Luckily only Jack has a vote, but I'm not sure he can accept such a radical change approach."

"Oh, you mean the large group intervention stuff?" Troy asked. "I hope he will. Last year I was involved in that type of change approach, and it really worked great."

"You what?" I exclaimed. "When were you involved in anything like that? Let's wait till we sit down; I want to hear this."

We sat down at Troy's regular table in the back of the room. He said, "So old Troy has some information that you might like to have, huh?" I was convinced he really was upset I hadn't invited him to join the team. "I thought I told you about my representing IRT on a big plastic supplier's reengineering effort?" He went on without waiting for my answer. "They used a 'whole scale change' approach, as they called it, bringing in customers, suppliers, and about half their plant in a major effort to shorten their entire supply chain cycle time. We must have had two or three hundred people at each of about four meetings, two days each—amazingly well orchestrated, and very productive. Their level of commitment impressed me. Now they're our best supplier. They never miss our need dates and react unbelievably to our never-ending problems. I copied you on my weekly reports where I raved about the approach. I take it you didn't read them. Jack sent some comments back, but I'm sure you were busier. He was just running the whole operation."

Sometimes it was hard to stay friends with Troy.

Troy smiled. "You know we're playing golf against Tim and Dick again Saturday. I hope you've been practicing your short putts. I still can't believe you missed that one on Monday. Hell, I'll bet it wasn't more than a foot and a half."

"Dammit, Troy, it was at least three feet."

Without acknowledging my protest, Troy switched topics. "I like Dick. He seems to have mellowed over the last couple of years. Never knew he didn't like Grant or Doyle. Good guy."

A few minutes before our nine o'clock meeting, I checked out the conference room and commandeered a front seat. I felt better now that I had an endorsement from someone who'd actually seen this participative change approach work. Everyone came in and sat in exactly the same places as before. I seemed to have gained some respect from the unthreatened members of the leadership team, but neither Nathan Jorgenson, Charles Osgood, nor Doyle gave me so much as an acknowledgement, which suited me just fine. Jack came in right at nine, spoke to my team in the back for a moment, and then walked to the front of the room.

Holding up *The Minding Organization*, he asked whether anyone had bothered to find and read it.

"You should," he added when only Carl and I raised our hands. He looked from one face to another. "It's about letting organizational improvements, or products, emerge from collective learning across the organization. It certainly supports Jon's knowledge-based development approach. It recognizes that knowledge can't be stagnant and that it resides across the entire workforce. Letting knowledge emerge must be our leadership mission."

Jack then sat in his usual spot. His comments had been typical of his style of management. Mainly he just asked questions and made observations.

He gestured to me to start the meeting. I walked to the front of the room and put up my first slide (Figure 8a).

"On Monday, I presented my report in response to Jack's request to understand why we're falling behind in several key business metrics. We concluded that over time we'd become too reliant on structure and process in our approach to product development. Our team looked at a number of key issues that our current initiatives would not, and could not, address. We also looked at the results from a National Center for Manufacturing Sciences consortium project and other studies that uncovered another paradigm, based not on the organizational structure, but on the knowledge of the individual workers. This has let

210

companies like Toyota excel where we are failing. Our team concluded that while our current philosophy couldn't resolve those same issues, the knowledge-based paradigm could. Our goal is not to look like Toyota, but to build our own environment based on the paradigms that have made them successful."

Development Environment
- The foundation for lasting change -

A Continuum

Structure-based	Knowledge-based
The basis of the engineering environment is the *structure of the operational activities*: procedures, control, compliance, related training	The basis of the engineering environment is the *knowledge of individual workers*: understanding of needs, information availability, responsibility, and teaming interaction
(Figure 8a)	

Charles Osgood said, "You do realize that several of us haven't bought into this new paradigm approach as being the answer. I just wanted you to know that."

I looked squarely at him. "Charles, I certainly realize that. I also realize that it's always hard to get people who've achieved personal success with one type of behavior to understand its impact on the company as a whole." I'd decided to be more confrontational with my three adversaries today. I was retiring in two weeks, so why hold back? It was working. Charles was obviously angry, but I thought I saw Jack starting to grin.

With that, I showed my next slide (Figure 8b).

"The key components of the change are four new elements that describe how we should be executing our product development processes. The first is 'Set-based Concurrent Engineering,' which is a way of examining multiple alternatives at a subsystem level. This provides a higher degree of redundancy, innovation, and involvement than our top-down approach, and it calls for replacing our administrative project management with technical entrepreneurial leadership. It also calls for replacing our ineffective top-down, task-based planning system with planning distributed to the engineers, making them responsible for their work. In fact, everything is geared toward letting the engineers be responsible for their personal performance to achieve the project goals. The advantages of this environment, intuitively, are clear to all but a few of you. The concern is, can we make it happen?"

The Key Elements of the Change

- **Set-based concurrent engineering**
  - *Multiple subsystem alternatives from all perspectives; combine; test; narrow; learn*
- **System designer entrepreneurial leadership**
  - *Clear technical leadership and focused responsibility*
- **Responsibility-based planning & control**
  - *Distributed planning & control based on key integrating events*
- **Expert engineering workforce**
  - *Competent personnel given responsibility for personal performance against project goals*

(Figure 8b)

Without waiting for more comments, I put up my next slide, to begin focusing on the changes required (Figure 8c).

"Here's a simple view of the process change we'll need as we move from our structural flow to one in which the system architecture emerges from the interaction of all the functional perspectives. Conceptually, this is the result of putting those four key elements from the previous page in place."

Nathan Jorgenson said with that little smirk, "And you really believe that our products will just magically emerge if we put those four elements in place."

"No, not magically," I replied. "Remember that the set-based process depends on a high level of design expertise operating in a logical process that continually evaluates and develops the pro-

The Product Development Change

Change from:

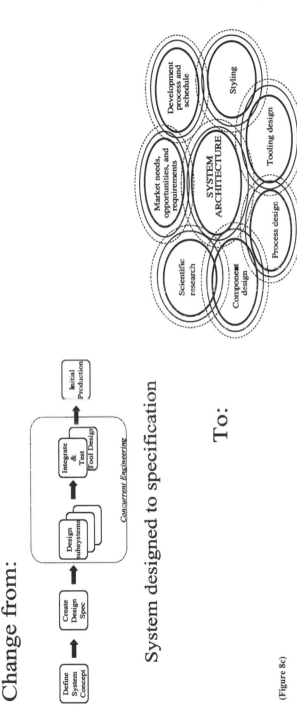

System designed to specification

To:

System emerges from subsystem possibilities

(Figure 8c)

duct from multiple perspectives. It's not magic, just design excellence." Now I'd ticked off the second of the trio. Good.

I put up the next slide, which was intended to make the large change gap clear to everyone (Figure 8d).

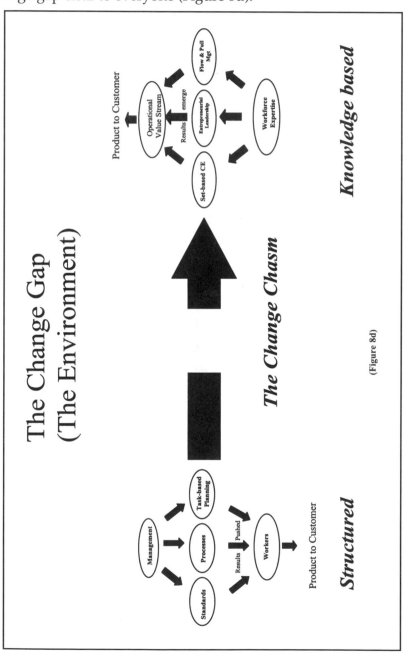

(Figure 8d)

"The last slide showed the process change, but realistically our entire cultural environment must change. The left side represents how our culture has developed over the years. Management *pushes* standards, processes, and detailed planning onto the workers to ensure they comply with our definitions of excellence. The knowledge-based environment, on the right, is one where the knowledge of all our workers is *pulled* by the key elements I already discussed. Yes, the change is huge, but it's doable, and how to do it is what I'll be discussing from this point on."

Wayne Tillotson said, "Jon, I like this view of the differences. In my opinion, you're right on. Over the last few years, we've definitely been pushing more and more structure onto our design teams. Many of our best people are also leaving. I can't believe part of it isn't that they're being smothered with constraints. Doyle, the PDSP document grows every year. Do we really need that much standard process?"

Doyle, who'd been quiet thus far, reacted predictably. "The PDSP grows only as we learn better ways of doing things. It only makes sense to add them to the process. You can always tailor them out."

"Yes," Wayne said, "but that takes time and effort, part of that eighty percent non-value-added labor. What's more, many of our best engineers don't believe your way is the best way for our projects."

I showed my next slide to start the change discussion (Figure 8c).

"Not surprisingly, we change our functions and processes the same way we design processes—with a lot of structure, a lot of administration, and knowledge from a small group of experts who have all the answers. These experts' and management's job is to convince everyone, or to mandate to them, that the changes be followed. Also not surprisingly, these changes seldom take hold. Eventually, they either just fade away or, worse yet, hang around for years, costing support dollars and aggravating people."

Doyle protested. "That's just not fair. Our compliance to the PDSP process is continually growing, so we know we're being successful in implementation."

Our Traditional Change Process Won't Work

- Too structural
- Too administrative
- Too little knowledge
- Too slow with 70% failure

The change process must mirror the change

(Figure 8e)

"Come on, Doyle," Christine said. "Surely you know everyone's just learning how to do creative accounting on the metrics. It's a game everyone plays at design reviews. I have to agree with Jon, we've had very poor success deploying new processes or quality programs."

"There is another way," I said as I put up my next slide, describing at a high level my recommended change methodology. It was critical that everyone understood the analogy between product development and organizational change (Figure 8f).

Approach

To use the knowledge-based philosophy to design the knowledge-based development system
  - Build from operational alternatives
  - Use the knowledge of our people
  - A few integrating events
  - Shared responsibility toward a single vision

(Figure 8f)

I let them read it, then said, "Robin Liebermann, from our Business Process Engineering team, introduced us to a change methodology that's been very successful in implementing organizational changes. It mirrors the knowledge-based product development process and builds operational alternatives from the bottom, instead of from the top down. It draws on workers' knowledge of their own jobs to define the required changes. It uses a few integrating events for decisions and planning. It's called the 'participative' methodology for change, and its success is well documented. The key to that success is the direct involvement of the people doing the work in the actual changes."

Jim Shipmann said, "But Jon, doesn't that break the fundamental rule that change has to be implemented from the top down?"

"No, not at all," I replied. "A top-down vision and a strong commitment to the change are critical. But that doesn't mean the change has to be designed at the top. How in the world can our administrative management, or a so-called expert team, define the workplace changes required? They don't have the experience or the knowledge. What we need is 'top-down vision' and 'bottom-up implementation.'"

"It sounds *too* simple," Christine said. "Doesn't there need to be some sort of system engineering team to glue it all together? Otherwise, couldn't it have the potential of being mob rule?"

"Actually, there is a change leader and a small integrating staff." I said. "They'll be responsible for putting substance around the vision, orchestrating the integrating events and documenting the results. I'll discuss this more in a few minutes."

Jack asked, "Didn't Troy Hoeller get involved with a supplier last year on some kind of a big change process? He seemed to like it, and you know Troy, he doesn't like much."

"Yes, he did," I said. Boy, was I glad I saw Troy this morning. "We're talking about the same approach he was so impressed with. Here's a conceptual view on how it works."

I showed my next slide (Figure 8g).

"The vision of the change and the fundamental principles of the knowledge-based development environment will be established from the top. From that point, all the details of the environment will be built from the bottom. Each organization will be involved from its own perspective. The overall environment will emerge from combining all those perspectives, but it must comply with all aspects of the vision. The change team leader and integration team will make sure it does. Their roles will be like that of Toyota's Chief Engineer."

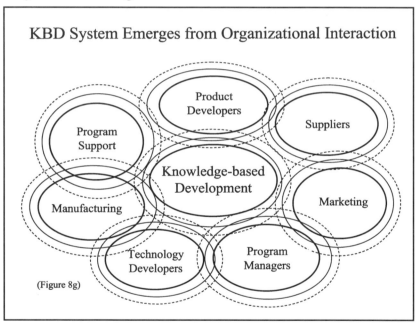

KBD System Emerges from Organizational Interaction

Product Developers

Suppliers

Program Support

Knowledge-based Development

Marketing

Manufacturing

Technology Developers

Program Managers

(Figure 8g)

Jim said, "But Jon, surely all the details from these many perspectives aren't going to just mesh naturally. Some will have to be modified to make it all work together. How is that done?"

"Through natural communication," I replied, "and eventually through integrating events where decisions are made about what works, what doesn't work, how things need to be combined, and what tests need to be made."

"And who makes those decisions?" he asked.

After yesterday's discussion, I'd expected this question and had thought more about the implications, so I said, "As I mentioned earlier, the change leader is responsible for maintaining the change vision. This should include the overall system design or architecture of the new system. However, the leader must carefully weigh when to delegate the operational details to the involved organizations. The ability of one person, or a team, to be able to anticipate, much less resolve, all of the organizational ramifications of a company-wide change would be very difficult. If set up properly, these integrating sessions can provide that mechanism. Organizational alternatives and test results can be addressed openly. Integration issues can be understood and resolved, and plans established for testing elements of the change. In reality, the design team for the new product development system includes not only everyone in product development, but also human resources, manufacturing operations, accounting, sales, and so on. In effect, the change leader must orchestrate all of this while both maintaining the system design and aligning broad participation in order to pull it off."

Jim replied, "I see the logic, but I'll believe it when I see it."

Robin answered for me from the back "It absolutely does work. I've seen it. The commitment of a knowledgeable and involved workforce sees to it. As Jon just said, the key is for the change leader, or chief change engineer, to know when to delegate."

Jim spoke again. "It seems that it'll take a lot of courage from upper management to follow this change approach."

"But remember," Robin said quickly, "it's upper management that sets the vision and ground rules."

Jim gave a slow nod, but it was apparent he wasn't totally satisfied. He said, "All right, let me repeat back what I think I heard—correct me if I misunderstood. The change leader is akin to the chief engineer and is the overall product development system designer. *But*, because of the breadth of the change, these large group integration sessions become an important tool for change.

They allow broad communication for decisions and knowledge, but more important, they pull active participation from all areas of the organization."

I nodded, slowly. His understanding was impressive.

Jim continued, measuring his words. "I assume these integrating sessions are also intended as decision-making events for inter-organizational issues, most of which will impact change issues. But they probably will not impact actual system design issues."

I nodded again. "Yes, generally. I'd say you're correct. But I suspect some overall system design decisions would be delegated to the integration sessions, or would evolve from them. It'll be the responsibility of the change leader to set this up properly. And he or she will need to be ready to react to surprises."

Wayne said, "This discussion is helping me understand the KBD process—see, I'm learning the acronym. The system designer, which is one of the four key elements, is the one who makes those 'integrating' type decisions, and that's why that role is so critical from a technical perspective."

"Absolutely," I said. Though I'd never really thought about it, it certainly made sense.

It seemed to me as though everyone in the room was becoming more comfortable with both the KBD environment and the participative change approach. Without waiting for more discussion, I put up my next slide (Figure 8h).

"This is our change plan and the key integrating milestones. The second milestone, the one after launch, establishes product development performance targets, and it defines a number of potential solutions for the entire knowledge-based system. Our team has defined our interpretation of the Toyota system, but there could be others or variations, too, that should be put on the table. Leading up to this milestone we will need to take care of education, assessments, and the defining of roles and responsibilities. The purpose of the first integration session will be to understand the options, discuss ramifications, and to plan

The Change Plan

A series of Integrating events

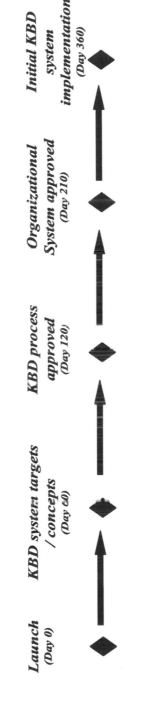

| Launch (Day 0) | KBD system targets / concepts (Day 60) | KBD process approved (Day 120) | Organizational System approved (Day 210) | Initial KBD system implementation (Day 360) |

With defined responsibilities for execution

- Integrating Staff: Change team (~8 people)
- Change Team: Large cross section from all aspects of product development (~200 peo

(Figure 8h)

evaluation details. The next milestone will establish our version of the set-based process and conceptual alternatives for the other three elements—system designer, expert workforce, and responsibility-based planning and control. The milestone after this, 'Organizational System Approved,' locks down the overall KBD system specifics, and the last one is the implementation of the new system within one of our business units. Each of the milestones, or integration points, will be set in concrete and will be large group sessions involving communication, reviewing, decision-making, and planning.

"The change leader, appointed by Jack, will have the overall responsibility for the design and implementation of the new system. We've already discussed this role and how it compares to the role of the Toyota chief engineer, as well as possible variances based on the uniqueness of corporate change. Okay?"

I glanced from one person to the next. Based on body language, I could see that most seemed to have accepted the change concepts, although maybe not all the details.

I decided to move on to the money slide (Figure 8i).

The Cost

- Integration Team (8peo X 12mo X 80%)
- Consultants (Lean / Change) (3peo X 12mo X 30%)
- Large Group Sessions (200peo X .5mo)
  - Four meetings to see results / make decisions
- Change Team (100peo X 1mo)
  - Prototypes / analysis / documentation of results

(Figure 8i)

"This is roughly what the costs are. We'll need a full-time integration team for the year of change. We estimate three consultants to be used about thirty percent of the time, one for leading the change meeting, and two who understand the knowledge-based development concepts. We'll have four large group meetings of an estimated 200 people, and another amount for prototyping. All totaled, that's the equivalent of about 24 full-time people."

Doyle quickly challenged this cost estimate as being too expensive.

I responded that it was less than his maintenance and enforcement cost for the PDSP initiative, and he just shrugged.

With no other comments, I showed the next slide, on the payback (Figure 8j).

The Payback

- ## Increased profits:
  - Potential of 4x productivity improvement
  - Reduced overhead rate
  - Increased market share
  - More products faster
- ## Reduced operational costs
  - Lowered initiative sustaining costs
  - Management consultants / new initiatives

(Figure 8i)

"I really don't have a good handle on how to calculate the return on our investment. But a quadrupled return on productivity alone will easily justify the cost. Even a doubled improvement would do it, as would the potential for overhead rate reduction, increased market share, and consistent products through reduced cycle times. All of the cost and return numbers will need to be worked in more detail, but I'm personally convinced the KBD approach will easily justify the expense."

Charles said with a smirk, "Pretty sparse justification."

"We've been spending a lot more each year on a lot less justification," I said. "And we do it year after year." I really disliked his predictable bullying style.

I put up my last slide (Figure 8k). I had no idea of how this would go over with Jack.

The Next Steps / Responsibilities

- Establish vision / constraints: Jack Holder
- Define / charter Integration team: Jack Holder
- Define integration events / timeline /   Jack Holder
  responsibilities:

(Figure 8k)

I said, "Getting started is really quite simple. We need to establish a vision for where we're going and what the constraints are. We need to establish the integration team that will start preparing for the first integration event. And we need to establish the timeline of integration events. This is my last chart. I realize we've given you mostly high-level justification for both the knowledge-based development environment and the participative approach to change. But we believe it's the right direction for IRT, one that can reverse our business metrics."

Doyle was the first up. "I like some of what you've presented. But we can start moving that way within our current initiatives. I'd like to propose that we see how we can integrate your ideas into the PDSP process. I'm sure we can find a small project that would be willing to try them."

Wayne quickly jumped in. "I disagree, Doyle. I don't believe it will integrate well at all into the PDSP process. You can't mix the methodologies."

I stood at the front of the room while the leadership team argued. Jack, as usual, just listened. Finally, Wayne—I was beginning to like him even more—proposed we break the impasse.

"I'd like to volunteer my unit to try Jon's recommendations. I personally like the potential, and I don't see that much risk. I do like the participative approach for change. It will allow direct involvement of the people doing the work. They'll find the right balance and will make it work."

Christine also volunteered to be involved.

Nathan Jorgenson, who headed our largest business unit, Military Products, agreed. "I like Wayne's suggestion. We can use his business unit as a pilot, evaluate how well it works, and then deploy as it makes sense through the rest of the business. Let's go with that approach." Nathan was used to getting his way. Everybody seemed to be nodding in agreement with him, and I was feeling that at least this would be a partial victory.

Then Jack got up, which is always my clue to sit down. I expected he'd jump on the bandwagon. He didn't.

"I might be an old country boy" he started. Damn, I thought to myself, whenever he's ready to unload on someone, he starts with that 'old country boy' routine. I doubted if anyone else in the room knew that, but it certainly made me very nervous. I was afraid he was going to trash the whole concept. I'm retiring and don't need this, I kept reminding myself.

Jack continued. "Let me see if I get this straight. The proposal is that we pilot both this new process and the change approach on Wayne's business unit while everyone else waits and watches. Am I the only one who sees a problem?" He waited for a few moments. Nobody had expected his reaction or question.

I must admit I was still very nervous about where he was going.

Jack started speaking again. "Some of you people are playing games. I don't like games." He paused again. You could have heard a pin drop.

I felt better. It looked like I wasn't his target.

"Nathan, you and Charles have no intention of changing, but you've got no problem playing the waiting game while all the focus is on Wayne. Why didn't you just say so? Doyle, we all know your motivation. Enough said. The approach you all suggest would be a disaster."

"First, we can't afford dual improvement approaches. We're already spending too much on our ongoing improvement initiatives. Look at our damn overhead rate. Second, we'll be sending the worst of all messages to the people—absolute indecision as to what our operational philosophy is. Some of you will take every opportunity to subvert the other approach, as will others whose careers are based on our current initiatives and not the success of the company as a whole. I talked to some people yesterday in the automobile industry about this lean, as they call it, approach to product development. Philosophically, there seems to be a lot of agreement on the principles. But I saw only limited commitment to change. They seemed to be okay with just kicking the tires. But they also confirmed that Toyota and Denso were the benchmarks for cost, quality, and time-to-market."

After another of his pauses, Jack continued. "The bottom line is that we're going to commit to this new paradigm, or philosophy, and move ahead quickly. We're also going to commit to Jon's proposal for change. What do we have to lose? Our people, whom I've been talking to a lot this week, don't trust any of our current initiatives. They just comply as best they can. This participative process for change will get them involved again. Where's the risk here? We will not have multiple improvement initiatives anymore. We'll have just one—to create a customer-focused, knowledgeable work force that will achieve ninety percent value-added productivity. Twenty percent cannot be tolerated.

"Again, I ask, where's the risk? I've also made up my mind that the issues Jon and his team discussed the other day must all be resolved if we're going to be successful. This knowledge-based approach logically will resolve those. Where's the risk? I don't really care whether we end up looking like Toyota. I only care that our people are back to being committed personally to the customer, that our project leaders have the freedom to please their customers, that we have schedules we adhere to, and that our engineers are the best in the business. Where's the risk? Anything we do to approach this will be positive. The only risk is to the many special-interest organizations that have built careers on establishing rules and standards. Any questions?"

He scanned the room, then added, "I assume Jon can give us a reading list. I want all of us to learn all these principles. My leadership team will be the strongest supporter of these changes as we move ahead. I hope each of you will be included."

The room remained very quiet. I suspected three people present were weighing their career options. At least I hoped so.

Turning to me, Jack said, "Jon, I think my first task is to name an integration team to begin preparation for the change, correct?"

I nodded, and he continued, "Would you consider delaying your retirement for a year and leading the integration team you suggested? I'll roll all our current initiative funding under you and your team's direction. I also have no problem with you hiring the consultants you need."

The obvious smiles on Jan's and Robin's faces and the scowl on Doyle's made the decision for me.

"Sure, I'll be glad to."

How could I lose? Even my wife would be happy. She had been dreading my retirement.

DISCUSSION

Our case study ends with the leader's commitment to create a knowledge-based development environment, to be achieved through the participative change methodology. Toyota has the best product development process in the automobile industry and arguably the best in the broader manufacturing business segment. The knowledge-based development environment mirrors the Toyota system, embodying the attributes that make it so successful. But it's only an interpretation. Trying to copy all the specifics of how Toyota operates would be very difficult and probably wouldn't fit other companies' cultures.

At the heart of the knowledge-based environment are workforce expertise, individual responsibility, technical leadership, and set-based concurrent engineering. Different companies can make use of each in many different ways. Letting the existing company culture adapt these concepts will work better than trying to adapt the culture to accept particular tools and procedures. Knowledge-based development is an operational philosophy, not a specific process.

In the case study, I also recommended that the KBD system be the foundation for actually making the change. There are many corollaries between the Toyota development system and whole-scale change methodologies that have proven very successful for corporate change. It seems logical to leverage learning by integrating the change process with the actual change itself. Chapter 9 will discuss the change process in more detail.

Through many years of observing and working in the worlds of product development and corporate change, the two messages in this book, the KBD process and participative corporate change, have been found to be highly successful by the few organizations that have applied it. Unfortunately, both seem to work against the prevailing corporate culture for development and change. Hopefully, I have shed some light on the possibilities.

Chapter 9

Transforming the Business
(The Power of the Workforce)

The Change Challenge

As was emphasized in the introduction, this book has two messages. The first, and more interesting, is the magic that makes the Toyota product development system so rich and unmatched in capabilities. The second, just-as-powerful message, is how to adapt the Toyota system's principles throughout an entire business. As I hope you now are fully aware, it's not about rearranging process steps, nor about new tools, nor about new metrics. And it is most certainly not about sticking Toyota's organizational nomenclature on the same old systems and processes.

Last year, while giving a training seminar, a manager at an auto supplier proudly told me that his company now had 'chief engineers' like Toyota—no changes in their administrative roles, mind you, just new names. Looking like Toyota is about working like Toyota—fundamentally redesigning the organizational underpinnings of the product development environment. That's why I resisted calling this book *Lean Development*, which implies simply an extension of lean thinking from manufacturing into development. Though it will undoubtedly improve the current process, there's no way a coordinated effort to systematically eliminate waste in development can recreate the Toyota development system.

It's also highly doubtful that trying to exactly replicate the Toyota development system will work. Toyota's process, organization, tools, standards, and training have all been evolving over the last half-century in an entirely different culture, and in most cases, an entirely different business environment. The change goal must be to understand the fundamental principles behind Toyota's success and to rebuild, customize, and evolve those principles to fit each company's culture. The heart of the Toyota development system is its ability to manage the collective knowledge of the engineering workforce to create an ongoing value stream of current products *and* to systematically create the new knowledge for future products. Creating this is the challenge.

I've been in the corporate change game for most of my career. On the surface, what I just described overwhelms all the traditional change methods. It can't be done by simply changing or eliminating process steps, or changing personal work procedures, or even changing organizational reporting.

Consider this. Changing American manufacturing's quality culture was probably the most successful large-scale change effort ever attempted. And it's taken twenty years from Juran, Crosby, and TQM through Six Sigma. It's also taken twenty years or so for manufacturing to evolve from inventory control, through just-in-time supply chain management, to lean manufacturing. And even after all these years and the obvious benefits, many companies still haven't made these important changes.

It will likely be every bit as challenging for American Industry to adopt the Toyota knowledge-based principles of product development. But it will also be every bit as important and beneficial. Yet, in light of engineering jobs moving overseas to countries with low-cost labor, it must not take twenty years to accomplish. It needs to happen now. In theory, this shouldn't be difficult. Adopting the Toyota development principles requires no new tools, no new operational methodologies, no new skills. It does require a major reemphasis on design fundamentals, a change that will be logical to a product development workforce and largely welcomed by them. In other words, nothing technical nor in anyway inherent to an organization prevents a company from quickly and effectively transforming.

There are two methods for implementing major change. The common approach is what I call the 'define and convince' model, in which an assigned expert (or expert team) defines the change specifics and convinces the rest of the organization to follow their recipe for change. This model works best in small companies, largely because of the close link between the company's leadership and its workers. But in large companies, this process is slow, seldom wins widespread buy-in, and often requires extensive infrastructure and procedural controls to maintain the change.

The other method is the 'participative model,' in which the leader defines the change goals and challenges the workforce to define and execute the changes. The process itself is a series of facilitated large-group sessions for convergence and decision-making, sandwiched around smaller group parallel activities for testing and learning. The power of this approach is the rapid assimilation of knowledge and buy-in across the organization. But it requires the leaders to trust the workers, not 'perceived' experts, with the details.

'Participative change' roles differ significantly from those in the 'design and convince' approach. The leaders are not 'order givers,' but participants in 'learning and decision-making.' Experts don't define specific changes, but rather, provide substantive knowledge. Workers are not 'change targets,' but full participants in learning and decision-making.

Although rarely used in manufacturing companies, 'participative change' is not a new change management philosophy. Scores of books espouse it as an approach for change. Appendix A lists recommended reading for understanding this methodology better. The books propose many tools and techniques for engaging the workforce. Tools and techniques may differ in style, but all are based on the imperative that the development workforce be fully engaged and involved in the change. This approach does require special facilitation skills for orchestrating the large group sessions. An organization's leader must understand the process and have the confidence to empower the workforce.

In Chapter 7, I compared this participative change method to the Toyota product development system. Both require leaders to set targets and make strategic decisions. Both require using workforce expertise to design the details. Both use hard milestones that depict key points of system integration. Both eliminate any need for administrators to control the process or define the results. A major difference is that Toyota assigns a chief engineer for the core product-level decisions, whereas the participative change process expects all key technical decisions to be facilitated at the integration events. I propose a hybrid approach for implementing the KBD environment. In this approach, a highly respected leader is assigned to be the chief change leader who makes core technical decisions. An alternative is to make a small team responsible. The large group integration sessions then become forums for understanding, defining, planning, and testing all integration issues.

Based on this, I will define the skeleton of a plan. Each company should work out the specifics. Working with the National Center for Manufacturing Sciences (NCMS), we've also developed and made available a cohesive support structure of external services. These include educational materials, forums for sharing knowledge, and consultation on subject matter and facilitation.

The Cycle of Change

Each chapter in this book has represented a critical element in an overall cycle of change. The following chart (Figure 9a) shows the cycle-of-change continuum. I do not wish to imply that each and every step in the chart must be followed in a structured way. But all the elements must be present in order for an effective, large-scale change to take place.

There *must* be a valid case for change, coupled with a call to action from the leadership. A baseline *must* be established to anchor the change and measure results. Opportunities for change *must* be identified, and then they *must* be evaluated and consolidated into an articulated view of the KBD system. The system concepts *must* be transformed into real operational capabilities. A clear commitment to change *must* be made. Sufficient resources *must* be assigned to actually transform the business. And the change itself *must* be completed quickly, generally in less than a year. Anything longer will appear as weak commitment and dissipate momentum.

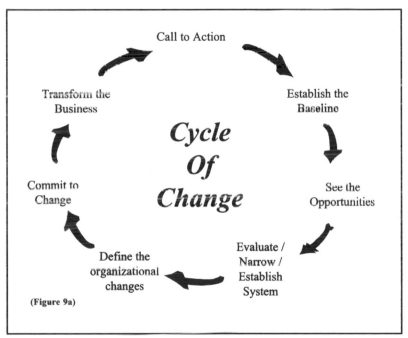

(Figure 9a)

Assuming an adequate job was done in selling you on the basics of the Toyota development system, it is certainly possible to believe that this cycle can be short-circuited; theoretically, the opportunities are already on the table and the vision already identified. That would be a mistake. Although this book does provide a jump-start concerning opportunities, ideas, and pitfalls, the people who make up your company still need to assimilate and internalize the concepts and adapt them to their circumstances. If you don't follow the change cycle, the potential that might be realized may not be reached, nor the momentum that might be built maintained.

Continuous Improvement versus Major Change

The cycle of change that I just described is for a major cultural organizational upheaval—in other words, a major discontinuity in operational philosophy within any of the core business processes. Certainly, the adoption of the Toyota-inspired product development system, as promoted here, qualifies as such a change for most companies. Another that also qualifies is lean manufacturing.

The question is often asked whether change models, such as the DMAIC Six Sigma model (Define-Measure-Analyze-Improve-Control), or Value Stream Mapping for lean waste removal, can be effectively used to achieve major change. In my opinion, these sorts of change models will never achieve a major shift in operational philosophy. This can only be accomplished through an conscious major redesign of organizational systems. However, I also believe that any or all of these continuous change models can and should be put in place as a part of any major change project. They will provide the means for continuous improvement.

Companies usually cannot absorb the overhead and the trials and tribulations of a host of major changes. At the same token, it is wishful thinking to believe that a company will evolve naturally into the Toyota style of environment. The best approach is to make the major change quickly and decisively, and then continuously improve operations via the ongoing change models.

The Change Process

I've discussed the participative change process many times throughout this book. A logical timeline is defined in Figure 9b and a list of milestones, activities, and timeframes suggested. This timeline is only a guide, not a detailed plan. It is critical, however,

Change Timeline

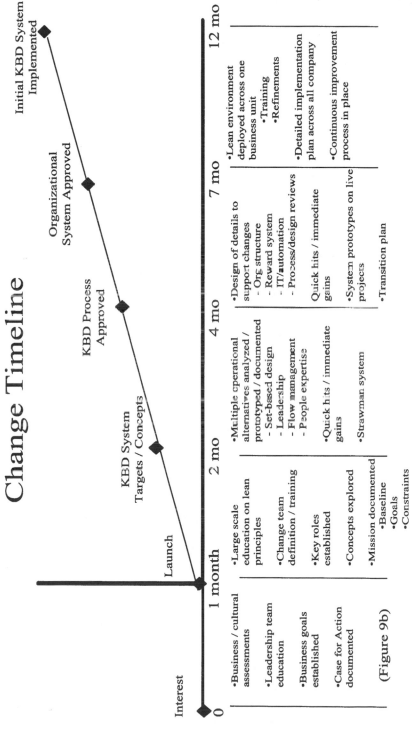

	Launch	KBD System Targets / Concepts	KBD Process Approved	Organizational System Approved	Initial KBD System Implemented
Interest					
0	1 month	2 mo	4 mo	7 mo	12 mo

Interest (0 – 1 month):
- Business / cultural assessments
- Leadership team education
- Business goals established
- Case for Action documented

Launch (1 month – 2 mo):
- Large scale education on lean principles
- Change team definition / training
- Key roles established
- Concepts explored
- Mission documented
  - Baseline
  - Goals
  - Constraints

KBD System Targets / Concepts (2 mo – 4 mo):
- Multiple operational alternatives analyzed / prototyped / documented
  - Set-based design
  - Leadership
  - Flow management
  - People expertise
- Quick hits / immediate gains
- Strawman system

KBD Process Approved (4 mo – 7 mo):
- Design of details to support changes
  - Org structure
  - Reward system
  - IT/automation
  - Process/design reviews
- Quick hits / immediate gains
- System prototypes on live projects
- Transition plan

Organizational System Approved (7 mo – 12 mo):
- Lean environment deployed across one business unit
  - Training
  - Refinements
- Detailed implementation plan across all company
- Continuous improvement process in place

(Figure 9b)

235

that firm system integration dates or milestones be set. It is also critical that they be spaced closely—no more than a few months apart. Momentum must be maintained.

I've also listed the types of activities to take place between milestones. These are given to help in defining the knowledge that must come together at upcoming integrating events.

I have added a pre-milestone called 'Interest' of one month's duration in order to highlight the importance of having the top leadership team on product development buy into the change process. This should include assessments of the current environment, education on the knowledge-based principles, setting the change goals, and organizing the change process. Whether the change is successful will depend largely on management's commitment to the change and the process, making this the most important time to use consultants as a catalyst for planning.

The defined milestones are actually system integration points. In the set-based process, these are the points at which forced narrowing of the possibilities takes place. These decisions might be made leading up to the meeting and reviewed at the meeting, or they may be made at the meeting. It is imperative that the dates be set early and that all activities support meeting these deadlines. The suggested milestone, 'KBD System Targets / Concepts,' has largely to do with education on principles. It also serves to get the options on the table. This book has described how Toyota uses knowledge as the basis for product development. Other techniques may also be employed to accomplish the same end. This milestone should insure those are put on the table along with an understanding of the specific targets for change.

The next milestone, 'KBD Process Approved,' is intended to lock down the set-based process. The principles of the KBD system are the set-based process, the system designer leadership, the planning and control system, and the expert workforce. I believe that establishing the set-based approach is the natural starting point to begin focusing on the other three principles.

The milestone, 'Organization System Approved,' fixes the details of how the principles are actually to be implemented—tools, policies, organizations. This is followed by the implementation of the entire system in the first business unit.

The milestone, 'Initial KBD System Implemented,' completes the process. This should include a review of the initial results of this first implementation and the identification of any corrections or changes to be made.

In the participative process recommended here, the integrating events (milestones) should be attended by a large cross section of all who are impacted by the change. As discussed, the purpose is to obtain broad participation, understanding, orchestrated feedback, and *decision-making*. These large sessions also make the progress highly visible, and they provide opportunities for visible support by upper management. This is important because maintaining change momentum is critical.

Let's turn now to decision-making. In a typical change process, the decisions for the new system are made by a few experts and deployed in an administrative manner. In the whole-scale change methodology, most change decisions are made at the integrating sessions through facilitators trained in gaining consensus. Here, I am proposing a hybrid. It is my opinion that a carefully selected change leader, or a small team, should be made responsible for implementing the KBD system. I believe, however, that it's critical that the leader make only the key narrowing decisions that insure the KBD principles are maintained. Operational details should be left to a broad cross-section of part-time volunteers. The integrating events provide the mechanism for achieving this.

Figure 9c contains a list of typical roles and responsibilities. The number of participants required depends on the company size and the objectives. The specifics are defined during the 'Interest' phase. The key roles are those of the change leader and the integrating team.

Roles & Responsibilities

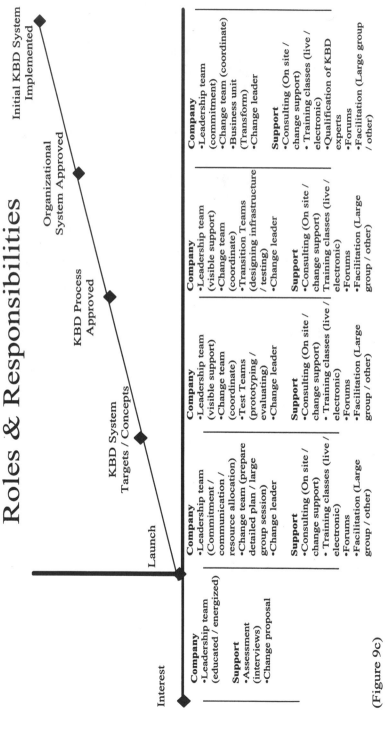

Interest

Launch

KBD System Targets / Concepts

KBD Process Approved

Organizational System Approved

Initial KBD System Implemented

Company
•Leadership team (educated / energized)

Support
•Assessment (interviews)
•Change proposal

Company
•Leadership team (Commitment / communication / resource allocation)
•Change team (prepare detailed plan / large group session)
•Change leader

Support
•Consulting (On site / change support)
• Training classes (live / electronic)
•Forums
•Facilitation (Large group / other)

Company
•Leadership team (visible support)
•Change team (coordinate)
•Test Teams (prototyping / evaluating)
•Change leader

Support
•Consulting (On site / change support)
• Training classes (live / electronic)
•Forums
•Facilitation (Large group / other)

Company
•Leadership team (visible support)
•Change team (coordinate)
•Transition Teams (designing infrastructure / testing)
•Change leader

Support
•Consulting (On site / change support)
•Training classes (live / electronic)
•Forums
•Facilitation (Large group / other)

Company
•Leadership team (commitment)
•Change team (coordinate)
•Business unit (Transform)
•Change leader

Support
•Consulting (On site / change support)
• Training classes (live / electronic)
•Qualification of KBD experts
•Forums
•Facilitation (Large group / other)

(Figure 9c)

The Tools of the KBD Process

I have a long personal history in the development of systems tools for the deployment of processes—CAD/CAM systems, manufacturing information systems, product data management systems. In this book, I have only made casual references to tools having to do with the implementation of the KBD process. This is because such tools are not emphasized by Toyota and the use of them is not considered critical for implementation. That said, I do believe that system tools can play a large role in implementation and should be considered—even emphasized—during the change process. Following is a list of logical system tools that could facilitate a good KBD process:

• A knowledge-based information system—a web-based repository for cross project knowledge. This would include format and search tools for standard formatted tradeoff curves.

• A responsibility-based planning system—a system that rolls up individual plans against set project milestones

• Project comparison matrix—a spreadsheet format that allows easy roll up of targets against possibilities; it would logically include standard profit model formats.

• Continuous Improvement process—Allen Ward has a model for continuous improvement, the LAMDA model, which should be reviewed as an ongoing process for waste removal within the KBD process.

I'm sure others exist or may evolve during the change process. The point I wish to make is that system tools can be an important part of the implementation process. But the tools must be in support of the KBD process, not the inverse.

The Lean Product Development Initiative

Obviously, this book cannot, nor can any collection of books, contain everything one needs to know in order to implement the knowledge-based development system in a particular company. This is why consulting should play a role. But consulting must only support the company change team. A consultant should not direct the change. No single expert knows enough about the principles of change management and best practices to be the single focal point. Outside experts can help the company optimize cost and leverage technology by being involved with the following:

- Assessments
- Collaborative projects / best practices
- Leadership forums
- Training (web-based / on-site)
- Facilitation
- Consulting (lean / knowledge-based / change management)
- Expert qualifications

NCMS is a non-profit company located in Ann Arbor, Michigan, that has extensive capabilities and experience in supporting collaborative projects in engineering and manufacturing companies. NCMS has formed the Lean Product Development Initiative (LPDI), as a source of support and help to companies transforming to the knowledge-based, or lean, operating philosophy. This organization can help a change effort by conducting in-house and electronic training and by providing a website suitable for sharing information. It can also offer broad experience in forming and facilitating projects and forums. NCMS has working arrangements with experts in all the required consulting roles, including the Toyota principles, assessments, and change management. The company is prepared to coordinate all consulting in support of implementation projects. Those considering making the change are urged to contact NCMS. See Appendix A for contact information.

Summary / Change Plan

This chapter discussed a sample project plan for transforming a business unit into a knowledge-based system. No two implementations will follow the same plan or end up with the same eventual system. But some fundamentals will be true in every successful transformation:

- The company's product development leader is committed and has set clear objectives and expectations for the change, and continually conveys those expectations.
- The product development workforce is totally involved in defining and making the required changes.
- The leader supports the changes and sustains the momentum.
- It happens fast.

The intent of the plan just outlined is to enforce these fundamentals. Other plans may as well, but they must be tested against these principles.

In this chapter, I have recommended a highly visible change process with published milestones and responsibilities that dramatically transform a company from one operational state to another—in other words, a revolutionary change. Some may wonder, can an evolutionary change work? Can a company systematically eliminate product development waste and eventually transform itself? In my opinion, the four cornerstones of the KBD environment are required for lasting change. These will not be created by an evolutionary approach. Throughout my career, I have seen many excellent process changes revert slowly to the old processes because the underlying organizational philosophies did not change. Let me urge you to beware of what may seem an easy way to change. Proceeding at a slow pace may be politically expedient, but seldom will this achieve significant results. Pragmatically, this might be the only way to get started at some companies, but in general, waste-removal efforts should be employed as a part of a larger change process.

Defining the payback is always an issue in improvement initiatives. What does it cost and when does it pay back? That's a valid question for equipment purchases, but is it really a valid financial question when faced with a totally different operational philosophy? What's the value of Six Sigma quality focus, or lean manufacturing? It might be whether you stay in business. The same is true with knowledge-based development, or lean development, if you prefer. What's the value of quadrupling engineering productivity? What's the value of cutting cycle time in half, or the value of development schedule consistency? My answer—you either leapfrog your competition or you keep up, but you must do something. Clearly, Toyota has proven that product development has the potential for a major leap in performance. American industry will evolve in this direction. The questions are how fast and who will lead.

Those are the questions that the leader should ask for his own company. Not "should we?" but "how far?" and "how fast?" The plan I outlined allows that level of decision. It must be addressed during the early stages of the change process.

Next Steps

I hope this book has piqued your interest. That's the first milestone. My recommended next steps are simple and painless. They are to understand the potential, understand the options, understand the approaches, and define the costs. Specifically:

- Contact NCMS or someone from the list of contacts in Appendix A.
- Arrange for more information through on-site consulting. This may take the form of a one-day overview/workshop with the product development leadership team. (To reduce costs and address product development leaders' common concerns, NCMS is investigating multi-company forums in selected cities.)

• Allow NCMS or another consultancy to conduct an on-site assessment of your company. One or two KBD/change consultants will interview key leaders and assess your process and culture for change. This will culminate with a recommendation to your leadership team as to scope, objectives, and a plan for the project. Two or three days will likely be required, as will the full-time involvement of your prospective change leader.

Final Thoughts

I hope you found this book helpful in that there may be vast, unrealized potential in your product development operations waiting to be tapped. Achieving this potential isn't black magic. It's simply a matter of commitment to the vision and letting the workforce fill in the details.

Appendix A

Selected Readings / Support

Knowledge-based Engineering is a term that was created within a project at the National Center for Manufacturing Sciences (NCMS) based in Ann Arbor, Michigan. The project was called 'Product Development Process-Methodology & Performance Measures.' The final report is available through their offices (www.ncms.org). Dr. Allen Ward is the leading proponent of Lean Product Development, which is his definition of the knowledge-based development environment. He was instrumental in guiding the NCMS project to its conclusions. Dr. Ward is associated with the Lean Enterprise Institute and is based out of the University of Michigan. He is dedicated to helping companies change to the lean philosophy. Dr. Ward has a number of training classes on the various components of lean as described in this book. They are offered through the University of Michigan and the Lean Enterprise Institute. I personally have worked with Dr. Ward on the NCMS project and on several other projects to promote the lean, or knowledge-based, development environment. Dr. Ward has written a pocket guide, "The Lean Development Skills Book," that outlines the concepts and skills involved. This is available at www.dollarbillcopying.com.

The participative change process is also known as Large Group Intervention, Whole Organizational Redesign, Conference Model, and Future Search. Which name is used depends on the consulting group using this tool. The approaches are similar and are based on energizing the entire organization to change. I would recommend the books, *Large Group Interventions: Engaging the Whole System for Rapid Change* by Barbara Bunker and Billie Alban, and *Whole Scale Change* by Dannemiller Tyson Associates as starting points for understanding this methodology.

There are a number of consultants who are trained in this process. Dr. Ward and I have talked extensively with people from Dannemiller Tyson Associates of Ann Arbor concerning their involvement. I believe that there is a natural marriage between this change methodology and the knowledge-based (lean) environment.

The Minding Organization by Moshe F. Rubinstein and Iris R. Firstenberg was a book I discovered after I'd finished the initial draft of this book. It is brilliant in setting down logically the need for an organizational environment such as Toyota's for maximum creativity and efficiency. My approach was much simpler: I observed the results and copied the mannerisms that yielded those results. With some work, I'd like to think that these authors could use the Toyota example to further refine the concepts.

CONTACTS:

NCMS
 Mike Gnam: mikeg@ncms.org
 http://lpdi.ncms.org

Mike Kennedy
 mn_kennedy@juno.com

Dr. Allen Ward
 allenward@comcast.com

Dannemiller Tyson Associates
 Al Blixt: alblixt@dannemillertyson.com

Appendix B

NCMS Project
(Product Development Process – Methodology and Performance Measures)

By Mike Gnam

Mike Gnam was the NCMS Program Manager. Here he presents an overview of the project that provided the original material for this book. The project, which initially was not focused on the Toyota system, provides interesting background and a broad perspective on the entire scope of product development.

Mike manages many of the collaborative R&D projects at the National Center for Manufacturing Sciences in the area of Management Practices. In addition to managing this project, he has managed a 15 company consortia project surrounding the multi-faceted aspects of Technology Management, which is now going into its sixth year. Prior to joining NCMS, Mike spent over 27 years in new product development, most notably as the Director of Engineering for a leading medical equipment manufacturer. At that company, he was the internal change agent for the Deming style TQM conversion of the enterprise.

In the last decade, companies concerned with improving time-to-market performance have given serious attention to understanding their product development processes. For improvement, companies have typically focused on specific areas of creativity and innovation such as concurrent engineering, automated design systems, and collaborative design. Although many companies have made significant improvements in time-to-market through these efforts, others have not. Even those that have are looking for the next generation of concepts to improve their development performance. To establish a competitive edge, companies continually evaluate new and innovative approaches for advancing their product development capabilities. Certainly, new product development lead times have been significantly reduced in recent years through Concurrent Engineering and Integrated Product and Process Design methodologies, and through the use of product design and PDM software. Of late, however, the pace of improvement in time-to-market (TTM) has slowed. What is needed is an insight on how other companies are dramatically faster, and then how to accomplish a "great leap forward" in improvement of TTM.

In 1997, the National Center for Manufacturing Sciences (NCMS) was approached by one of its member companies, GM/Delphi (now Delphi), for assistance in addressing the problem described in the preceding paragraph. NCMS is a not-for-profit consortium of member companies whose role is to form collaborative R&D efforts to advance the state-of-the-art in manufacturing enterprise practices and technologies. After several discussions with GM/Delphi, it was decided to seek other member companies to form a collaborative project to leverage the resources of all.

NCMS recruited additional project participants, and after several months a project was launched to address these issues. Project participants for this consortia project were GM/Delphi (Project Champion), Texas Instruments DSEG (now Raytheon), Cincinnati Milacron (now Cincinnati Machine), Ortech, Sandia National Labs, and United Technologies Automotive (now Lear).

The project participants believed that understanding engineering organizational performance and effectiveness was probably the next frontier for competitive advantage. Furthermore, the themes of creativity and innovation, concurrent engineering, math-based engineering, and automated design tools, while still key to winning, are not sufficient to attain a distinct competitive advantage. Therefore, attacking the issue of engineering organizational performance through understanding product design paradigms could be a significant breakthrough for achieving dramatically improved performance.

The project leaders believed that a deep investigation into the product design paradigms could uncover differences in the fundamental philosophies and approaches for design that separate the winners from the losers. The key questions are:

- How do companies design products successfully?
- What is the mental mindset of the designers in a world-class organization?
- What are the core values of the design group of such an organization?
- Are there fundamentally different techniques to design products?
- What is a successful model for the process of product design?
- What are the identifiable factors (drivers) that impact and influence the performance of the above design model?
- What are good measures of the effectiveness and performance of the product design process?
- Can all of the above factors be captured and described in an overall world-class paradigm description?

Uncovering the answers became the focus of the project.

The project ended in 1999 and was deemed very successful by its participants. While it was not the intent of the project to study the Toyota system per se, the investigations indicated that the greatest amount of the knowledge that was being sought could be attained by thoroughly studying the Toyota design "paradigm." Consequently, the project contracted with Dr. Allen Ward, who had spent five years, including much of his time in Japan at Toyota, studying the Toyota system and processes. Our project leader was attracted to Dr. Ward from his published article "The Second Toyota Paradox." Much of the findings and conclusions of this NCMS project were derived from Dr. Ward's efforts, both from his research in Japan, and as a contracted consultant to our project team.

The core of the findings of this project was a set of matrices of over 50 different paradigms that were documented by the project team. These matrices are presented here.

Process-Based Paradigms

Process Functions	Identified Operational Paradigms					
Solution search and Convergence	Fast-System Build	Set-based	Requirements Flow-down	Incremental Development	Modular Application	
System Architecture Management		Leader-Responsible	Platform	CORE team Design	Systems Engr Based	
Project Planning and Control	Central task oriented CPM, PERT	Decentralized streams	Pipe Line	Critical Chain	Phase Gate	Modular based
Specification Management	Test to Spec	Layered Transformation	Emergence			
Physical Prototyping & Testing	Validation focused	Verification focused	Decision making / Learning			
Performance Assurance & Control	Bureaucratic	Direct-responsibility	Team-work	Metric based	Specialist based	
Automation	Analysis Based	Parameter Based	Compiler Based	Platform Based	Generative	

Organizational-Based Paradigms

Organizational functions	Identified Operational Paradigms						
Leadership	Functional	Coordinating committees	Team	Project Managers	Powerful genius	Expertise based	Customer
Communication	Cross-functional Co-location	Functional co-location	Electronic / virtual co-location				
Personnel Management	Boss centered	System oriented	Market/reputation oriented	Potential-based	Qualification oriented		
Supplier Relationships	Design to contract	Partnership	Select from Catalog	Build to Print	Fee for Service		
Customer Relationship	Design to contract	Partnership	Design to catalog	Service for Fee			
Business-wide Resource Management	Functional Assignment (budgeting)	Project Owned	Business Prioritization	Process Owner			
Process Design / Standardization	Imposed	Learning-based	Metric-based				

Cultural-Based Paradigms

Cultural functions	Identified Operational Paradigms				
Orientation to Action	Advocate	Hands-on entrepreneur			
Orientation to Learning	Model optimization	Learning			
Decision Making Approach	Political	Intuitive	Economic model		
Adversity Management	Autocratic conversion	Corrective action team (SWAT)	White knight (internal /external consultant)	Increased focus / meetings	
Business Improvement / Change Management	Top-down directed	Participative change	Continuous improvement	Business process reengineering	Continuous flow development

The paradigms are mapped against key product development functions, with each representing an operational philosophy discovered for successful companies to execute that function. The paradigms were broken into three categories – those that impact process functions, those that impact organizational behaviors, and those that impact the culture of the work environment. The most interesting aspect was how the paradigms were combined at different companies to create the overall product development process. The Toyota grouping of paradigms, along with their clear success, became the focus of the project. In all cases, each of the paradigms named have a complete description of their meaning including performance measures. These are contained in the final report and are outside the scope of this appendix.

At the conclusion of the project, a final report was issued and an NCMS workshop created to convey the findings to others. The workshop included a blending of the principles found in the project with basic change management methodologies and an assessment mechanism, in order to help companies make the required paradigm shift. Subsequent to the project, the author, Mike Kennedy was inspired to write this book and, in conjunction with NCMS and Dr. Ward, is creating a family of services surrounding these findings. These are summarized in this book.

The author of this book, Mike Kennedy, was one of the founding members of this consortia project. At the time, he was with Texas Instruments, Defense Supply Electronics Group, a company with an established, and excellent, product development process. Being a leader in their field, TI wanted to make even more significant improvements, and thus they joined this project. Mike was a valuable contributing member of the project, until his retirement from TI, which unfortunately for the project team, came during the second half of the project time span. Fortunately, the team was able to contract for his services on the project, and Mike continued his valuable contributions to the project's conclusion.

Index

Index